THE ADVANCE OF
THE ENGLISH NOVEL

THE ADVANCE OF
THE ENGLISH NOVEL

BY

WILLIAM LYON PHELPS

LAMPSON PROFESSOR OF ENGLISH LITERATURE AT YALE
MEMBER OF THE NATIONAL INSTITUTE OF ARTS AND LETTERS

AUTHOR OF "ESSAYS ON MODERN NOVELISTS,"
"ESSAYS ON RUSSIAN NOVELISTS," ETC.

NEW YORK
DODD, MEAD AND COMPANY
1916

To
HENRY A. BEERS

PREFACE

Of this book, all the chapters except the last appeared originally in the *Bookman;* the last was printed in the *Yale Review* for July 1916.

My sketch of the advance of the novel in English includes two centuries. I have laid the chief stress on recent and contemporary writers, although it has been impossible even to approach completeness of treatment. Many novelists are omitted that may seem important; but the book is a record of personal impressions and opinions. I shall be glad if some individuals feel the pleasure of recognition, the pleasure of opposition, and a stimulus to further reading.

W. L. P.

Yale University,
Tuesday, 23 May 1916

CONTENTS

THE ADVANCE OF
THE ENGLISH NOVEL

THE ADVANCE OF THE ENGLISH NOVEL

CHAPTER I

PRESENT STATE OF THE NOVEL

The present state of the novel—its immense popularity—
the rise in its respectability—definition of a good novel—
the penalty of popularity—reasons for this popularity—
books sold under false pretences—distinction between
"romance" and "novel"—the philosophy underlying realism
and romanticism—the strength of realism—the vicious circle
in all art.

THE beginning of the twentieth century wit-
nessed the predominance in literature of the
novel. More copies of novels were in circulation than all other kinds of books put together.
It took two centuries to bring about the consum-
mation; and at this moment the novel is still
supreme. Nothing threatens its hegemony except the growing vogue of the printed play, accompanied as it has been by a blizzard of critical
works on the stage. We cannot help noticing

1

how many professional novelists have become
professional playwrights.   Does this mean that
the drama has really awakened at last, refreshed by a sound sleep of three hundred
years?   Does it mean that the dying prophecies
of William Sharp and Bronson Howard are to
become fact, and the next generation is to express itself mainly in dramatic dialogue, as in
the days of Elizabeth?   Or is all this play-mak-
ing simply one more florescence from the root
of all evil?   Has the same quick-return fever
that has shaken the souls from so many bodies in
business smitten the vast army of literary specu-
lators with drama delirium?

No accurate answers can yet be given to these
questions; but to those professional students,
critics and teachers of literature who are as
eagerly interested in contemporary production
as are teachers of science and economics, the literary movements of the next twenty years are
going to be well worth watching.   Meanwhile
the present proud height of the novel's popularity and influence makes an excellent platform for
the observer; he cannot only look about him; he

has a fine chance to look back, and if he is mentally alive, he cannot help looking forward.

There are fashions in the array of thoughts as there are fashions in corporeal coverings; and as it would be a bold undertaking to explain the causes of the time-variations in the length of men's coats and the diameter of women's hats, so even the most philosophical historian cannot fully account for the occasional predominance of certain literary forms. Even some literary *material* actually vanishes; scholastic speculation, that filled many folios, seems extinct. But the chief material of literature is human nature, which never changes; poets, dramatists, novelists, satirists focus their attention on "man's thoughts, and loves and hates." It is the fashion of expression that varies; it is rather interesting to reflect that not merely the mob of professional scribblers, who produce what to-day is, and to-morrow is cast into the oven, but inspired men of genius interpreted human life by means of the drama and the sonnet in 1600, by the heroic couplet in 1700 and by the novel in 1900. Twentieth century publishers are not

eagerly looking for theology in verse; yet two
hundred years ago theological poetry was a sure
card. Pope's *Essay on Man* sold off as sen-
sationally as Winston Churchill's *The Inside
of the Cup*. Pope and Mr. Churchill had one
thing in common besides success—an accurate
flair for public taste. I dare say that Pope
would be a clever realistic novelist were he alive
to-day—for he would know his market now as he
knew it then. In his time theological verse was
so much in demand that Samuel Boyse, who
usually wrote in bed, his frequent sprees giving
the pawn-broker possession of his garments,
composed a poem on the nature of the Deity, being forced—unhappy artist—to produce something that would sell. A similar predicament
would to-day drive his energies into a quite different channel. Boyse's poetry is read no
more; and he would have followed his works
were it not that Dr. Johnson liked him and used
to go about collecting sixpences to redeem his
clothes, thus giving temporary decency to his
body and immortality to his name. The reading
public in those days was patrician; in the latter

half of the nineteenth century, when the ability
to read ceased to be any more of a distinction
than the ability to breathe, the novel reached
the climax of popularity. For the novel is the
most democratic form of literature, easily
adaptable to minds of high, low and no intelligence.

The extraordinary popularity of the novel
toward the close of the nineteenth century is
proved by its sudden conquest of the American
stage. The relation between acted play and
published romance that had been one of the
most notable features in Elizabethan literature
again came into being—with just the opposite
emphasis and for a totally different reason.
The Elizabethan dramatists—except Ben Jonson—did not dream of inventing their plots;
their business, as some one has said, was not
creation, but translation. They hunted for
plots, not in their own brain, but in contemporary fiction; they selected a story, adapted it for
the stage, and in many cases gave it permanent
beauty. The only reason why many Elizabethan prose romances are still read is because

Shakespeare glorified them by his genius; Tolstoi being the only person who has maintained that the originals were better than the dramas. The playwrights took this material, not because it was popular, but because it was convenient; and the custom lapsed with the extinction of the Elizabethan stage. It was resumed, however, in 1894; and for ten years flourished mightily, being finally killed by the American sense of humour. Two prodigiously popular novels appeared in 1894: *Trilby* and *The Prisoner of Zenda*. They were quickly transferred to the stage, where thousands of people greeted the incarnation of their favourite characters with childish delight. The "dramatised novel" became a fad; every "best seller" was certain to take dramatic form, not because it contained germs of drama but because it was the thing everybody was talking about. Each theatre manager in New York employed men who made dramas with scissors and paste; and one director said frankly that the natural adaptability of the particular novel had nothing to do with the case so long as it was popular; he had

a man on a salary who had become so skilful
that he could make a play out of the city direc-
tory, were there any demand for it. It is seldom in the history of literature that the popularity of a certain form becomes so extensive
as to conquer another form with which it has
really almost nothing in common; in this instance the drama for a decade became the slave
of the novel; and the fact is worth recording as
showing the triumphant vogue of the latter.

The advance of the novel in popularity was
accompanied by an automatic rise in respectability. A hundred years ago novel reading was
thought by many to be positively wicked, classed
with that unholy trinity—cards, dancing, stage-
plays. The mother of Thomas Carlyle read
only one novel in her life, Goethe's *Wilhelm
Meister;* and she read that because her son
had translated it, the best of all reasons, from a
maternal point of view, for making an exception. Could Goethe by any possibility have
imagined in the course of its composition that it
would be read by such a woman? Yet John
Carlyle wrote to his brother Thomas: "She is

sitting here as if under some charm, reading
Meister, and has nearly got through the second volume. Though we are often repeating
honest Hall Foster's denouncement against
readers of 'novels,' she still continues to perse-
vere. She does not relish the character of the
women, and especially of Philina: 'They are so
wanton.' She cannot well tell what it is that
interests her." Indeed, from Jane Austen to
Henry James, responsible novelists were on the
defensive. In the fifth chapter of *Northanger
Abbey* we are told that two girls:

shut themselves up to read novels together. Yes,
novels; for I will not adopt that ungenerous and im-
politic custom, so common with novel writers, of de-
grading, by their contemptuous censure, the very performances to the number of which they are themselves adding; joining with their greatest enemies in
bestowing the harshest epithets on such works, and
scarcely ever permitting them to be read by their own
heroine, who, if she accidentally take up a novel, is
sure to turn over its insipid pages with disgust. . . .
Let us leave it to the reviewers to abuse such effu-
sions of fancy at their leisure, and over every new
novel to talk in threadbare strains of the trash with
which the press now groans. Let us not desert one

another—we are an injured body.   Although our productions have afforded more extensive and unaffected
pleasure than those of any other literary corporation
in the world, no species of composition has been so
much decried.   From pride, ignorance or fashion, our
foes are almost as many as our readers; and while
the abilities of the nine-hundredth abridger of the
History of England, or of the man who collects and
publishes in a volume some dozen lines of Milton,
Pope and Prior, with a paper from the *Spectator* and
a chapter from Sterne, are eulogised by a thousand
pens—there seems almost a general wish of decrying
the capacity and undervaluing the labour of the novelist, and of slighting the performances which have
only genius, wit and taste to recommend them. . . .
"And what are you reading, Miss ——?"   "Oh, it
is only a novel!" replies the young lady; while she
lays down her book with affected indifference, or mo-
mentary shame.   "It is only *Cecilia,* or *Camilla,* or
Belinda"; or, in short, only some work in which the
greatest powers of the mind are displayed, in which
the most thorough knowledge of human nature, the
happiest delineation of its varieties, the liveliest effu-
sions of wit and humour, are conveyed to the world
in the best-chosen language.

Twenty-five years ago Henry James thought
it necessary to insist on the "dignity" of the
novel.   The best novelists are really historians,

and the novel is history. Or, if one is unaffected by the challenge of truth, Mr. James pleaded for the worth of the novel in art. He declared that a picture was not expected to apologise for itself, why should the novel? Our Canadian contemporary, Mr. Leacock, who is a professor of political economy, rather indignantly denies the supposition that his humorous extravaganzas are the offshoots of leisure hours. Quite the contrary he affirms to be true, saying that any one can consult columns of statistics and rearrange them, but to write a work of pure imagination requires a much higher quality of mind and much more serious effort.

When I was a child my mother would not permit me to read novels on Sunday; and yet, some thirty years after that period, I received a letter from a woman who was very old, a bed-ridden invalid, and the widow of a Baptist minister (the three qualifications are not arranged as a climax); she wrote, "Thank the Lord for novels!"

If one indulges in a little analysis, one sees that the respectability of the novel was naturally

forced to rise with its popularity—not because
of a more general liberality in pleasures, a
weakening of the consciousness of sin, an increased flippancy in all life's habits and conventions; no, the rise in respectability came for just
the opposite reason. When any literary form
is predominant, the majority of writers are compelled to write in that form, simply because it is
the surest way to secure the two things that
nearly every writer wants—fame and cash.
The supremacy of Elizabethan drama forced
most of the great writers of that age to put their
ideas and imaginings into the dramatic form;
which is one reason why the Elizabethan drama
is so wonderful as poetry and so wretched as
drama. Of all those towering men of genius,
Shakespeare alone holds the stage to-day, and
only a small fraction of his plays are commonly
acted.

During the last years of the nineteenth century the novel became so popular that many
professional writers chose that method of expression, whether they had any natural love for
it or not, and even when they were totally ignor-

ant of the novel as an art form. All over the world thoughtful authors joined the ever-swelling ranks of the novelists. The result was, of course, that serious readers, men and women who were determined to read works that reflected the great movements in modern thought, were compelled to read novels. Clubs were organised all over the country to study contemporary fiction, courses on the novel in college curricula ceased to attract outside attention, and critical works on the subject multiplied abundantly.

This vast popularity of the novel was and is by no means an unmixed blessing. Indeed, with reference purely to the *art* of fiction—a great and noble art—it has been fraught with disaster. If I were forced to make a definition, I should define a high-class novel in five words—*a good story well told*. How rarely do we find a perfect illustration! The number of people who are seeking in the welter of contemporary books to find ''good stories''—stories that shall at once be interesting, charming, clever, decent, and that shall not be treatises on politics, religion or sociology—the number of such earnest seekers after amusement is pathetic. They want entertainment, and what are they doing? Many are turning from "novels" to history, biography, letters and essays to find it. Every man and woman with any pretension at all to a knowledge of literature is constantly besieged with this question: "Where can I find a really good story?"

For if a true novel be a good story well told, it is certain that the majority of so-called novels are not stories at all: of the saving remnant, only a few are good stories: and still fewer are well told. The great bulk of modern fiction may be divided into two classes—those that are merely rambling accounts of the lives of uninteresting characters, and those that are treatises on aspects of modern thought. Among the "best sellers" of the past thirty years only a small number could possibly be classified as artistic novels. Edward Bellamy was deeply interested in socialism, and its earnest advocate as well; in 1860 he would perhaps have written a tract embodying his arguments, but coming at

a later time, he called his treatise a novel, and
named it *Looking Backward*. Mrs. Ward has
never written a novel in her life, and only once
came near it, in *David Grieve*. But she is a
serious, earnest, thoughtful, deeply read woman,
with a passion to improve the world: she once
wrote a treatise on religious reform, and called
it *Robert Elsmere*. As people are more interested in religion than in any other subject in the
world save two, her book had a prodigious success—exactly paralleled a short time ago by
Winston Churchill's *The Inside of the Cup*.
For many months after the day of its publication this work was selling at the rate of five
hundred copies a day; yet, with the possible
exception of the curate, there was not a living
character in the book, there was no real story,
and none of the charm of fiction. But there
was a timely and earnest discussion of the modern creed and the modern work of the church,
with a plea for liberalism. Suppose one is interested in the question—Have we a right to kill
our friends when they are suffering acutely from
a hopeless disease?—one may be referred to

Edith Wharton's work on the subject, called *The Fruit of the Tree.* The fact that in this particular instance the woman who did kill her friend to save her from suffering subsequently married the friend's husband, is merely a matter of detail, and should not be permitted to distract our attention from the main theme. All of these "novels" remind me of the way I was once decoyed by a Sunday school book. I looked over the catalogue, and my youthful attention was arrested by the title *Putnam and the Wolf.* Thinking I should witness a rattling good fight, I drew out the book, and in the calm of the Sunday afternoon began to read. This was the first sentence: "As General Putnam descended into the cave to fight with the fierce and savage wolf, so should we all struggle with the demon of intemperance." And there was not a further allusion to either Putnam or the wolf in the entire work. "Money under false pretences" is a mild term for such literary dexterity; but it can now be paralleled in every publisher's list of forthcoming works of fiction.

The production of literature and the various

forms that it assumes are, of course, chiefly
governed by our old friend in the study of
political economy—the law of supply and demand. What, then, has caused the sharp demand for novels which has made the supply increase in a cumulative progression since 1850,
and which accounts for such a vast body of
essays, sermons, theses, arguments, scientific
treatises, masquerading as works of fiction? It
is, I think, the enormous increase of high
schools. Formerly the number of people for
whom reading was either a refuge or a stimulation was comparatively small; toward the close
of the nineteenth century millions of people
discovered the pleasure or the anæsthetic of
books. I do not refer to college professors,
ministers, journalists, etc., who make their living by reading books and then writing or speaking about them; no, I mean people engaged in
useful occupations, who work hard during the
day, and who read anywhere from six to fifteen
hours a week for pleasure. Most of these read
for a mental change of air, for rest, relaxation,
for refuge from sorrow, for relief from care,

possibly to get to sleep o' nights—this vast
army of readers demand, of course, something
entertaining, something that can be guaranteed
to divert the mind; and the novel has risen by
leaps and bounds to satisfy this particular
daughter of the horse-leech.

It is somewhat unfortunate, in discussing the
history of English prose fiction, that we cannot
make a sharp distinction between the words
"romance" and "novel." We ought to mean
by "romance" a story where the chief interest
lies, not in the characters, but in the events; as,
for example, *Quentin Durward*. By the word
"novel" we should denote a story where the
principal stress falls, not on the succession of
incidents, but on the development of the characters; an excellent illustration would be *The
Mill on the Floss*. Occasionally a man of genius has made a splendidly successful fusion of
the two, as in Thackeray's *Henry Esmond*—
which, if a secret ballot could be taken, might
possibly be voted the greatest work of fiction
in the English language. In 1785, at the flood-
tide of the English Romantic Movement, Clara

Reeve attempted to draw a distinction between the two words: "The novel is a picture of real life and manners, and of the times in which it is written. The romance, in lofty and elevated language, describes what never happened nor is likely to happen. The novel gives a familiar relation of such things as pass every day before our eyes, such as may happen to our friend or to ourselves." It will be observed that her distinction is not the same as the one I have suggested as desirable. I do not think the main difference should be one of style, nor do I think romances should include only those works which deal with fantastic or impossible adventures; for such a nomenclature would leave no place at all for those works of fiction that deal with historical events and personages in a manner that is meant to be scrupulously accurate. Such works, according to Clara Reeve, and all historians who follow her, could not possibly be either romances or novels. What are they, then?

When one considers such difficulties as these, one is, after all, reconciled to the generally prevailing loose use of the word "novel," which means simply any work of prose fiction. Definitions are dangerous; no sooner have you got your definition stated in a manner that appears to you sound and unassailable than some awkward questioner will want to know what you are going to do with such and such a concrete instance, which most certainly exists, and which refuses to conform to your artificially made standard. Creative writers are more interested in the inherent truth and beauty of their compositions than they are in their possible classification under established forms. A man who writes for the stage does not care very much if all the critics refuse to call his composition a play so long as the theatre is packed night after night and audiences are spellbound. It is better to have it indefinable and impressive than to have it a perfect illustration of the rules without the breath of life.

Still we can, I think, by remembering that romances contain incident and novels analysis, find such a distinction useful. One of the greatest of all English romances is *Lorna Doone;* and

its author, in his original preface, remarked:
"This work is called a 'romance,' because the
incidents, characters, time and scenery are alike
romantic. And in shaping this old tale the
writer neither dares nor desires to claim for
it the dignity or cumber it with the difficulty
of an historic novel." There you have the real
essence of romanticism—liberty. The romantic drama and the romantic story are essentially
free—free of all rules, and not to be measured
precisely by canons of criticism or standards
of fact. Mr. Blackmore did not care to verify
any statement or any person in his work; but
he meant to write, and did write, a good story,
a genuine romance. For *Lorna Doone* is surely
a romance, as *Barchester Towers* is surely a
novel.

For my part, as a tireless and catholic reader
of fiction, I do not much care whether I read
romances or novels. I have never had any of
Mr. Howells's contempt for romance. I have
more contempt for a badly written realistic
novel than I have for a well-executed, wildly
exciting romance. I had rather hear a good

melodrama than a stupid play founded on fact.
But the theories underlying romantic and realistic fiction are diametrically opposed, and
might be compared to two opposite methods of
treating a hospital "case." The romanticist
and the realist agree that all men and women,
no matter how apparently healthy, are suffering from an incurable disease—life. In addition to being doomed—every one of us—most
of us are not any too comfortable in our prolonged illness. Our days are filled with small
aches and pains, little vexations, frustrated
hopes, with every now and then a calamity or a
disaster of serious magnitude. Our appearance, ability and resources during the progress
of our disease are just ordinary, without any
positively striking characteristic. The world is
made up of average men and women, whose
lives are filled with trivial events. Your realist is a homeopath; because persons and hap-
penings are for the most part commonplace,
novels should be the same; they should exhibit
commonplace people, and extraordinary incidents should be barred. Let all novel readers

find the truth of life accurately reflected in art, and art will be a real antiseptic. Your romanticist, while agreeing in the diagnosis, insists on an absolutely opposite remedy. Because life is rather stupid and commonplace, art should be just the contrary. Novels should save us from ourselves, by taking us into a refreshingly different world. Romances should act on our nerves exactly as a change of air—to borrow Stevenson's phrase—acts on the bodily health. Without the slightest jar in the transit, we escape from our environment, meet marvellously strong men and radiantly beautiful women, who, after passing through thrilling adventures, reach a paradise of wedded love. The novelist remoulds the sorry scheme of things nearer to the heart's desire. We return to the daily task refreshed in spirit, with the blessed knowledge that the first half-hour of leisure can take us back to the world of beauty.

While the philosophies underlying realism and romanticism are thus diametrically in opposition, it must be confessed that, however alluring and diverting the field of romance may be, the realist makes in the end a deeper and more lasting impression on the mind. Suppose, for example, Blackmore had supplied a different ending to *Lorna Doone,* as some misguided critics would have preferred. It will be remembered that at the wedding in the tiny church Carver slips in with a gun and shoots the bride; she lingers for a page and a half, and recovers. Now, suppose she had succumbed. The reader would doubtless have wept; then shortly have dried his tears with the sound reflection that all this never happened, and that it is silly to weep over the fate of even so attractive a girl as Lorna, since she never existed. We come to ourselves at the end of a sad romance, as we leave the opera house after the curtain of *Königskinder* to eat a good supper, or as we awake from a horrible dream, and hear the reassuring trolley car go by. But the effect brought by a realistic novel cannot be thus summarily blotted out; in fact, it cannot be blotted out at all, except by the slow and unconscious method of forgetting it.

When one finishes *Esther Waters,* one cannot say, "Pshaw, this is all a dream!" because it is not a dream, and we feel certain that the selected cases are accurately typical of millions.

Every sincere novelist, poet and dramatist hopes that his created illusion will endure; all have a well-founded fear of importunate facts of life that may erase the impression made by the eloquence of art. The dramatist wishes that between the acts the audience would remain in their seats, discussing the probabilities of the next act in awestruck whispers; but the women indulge in social gossip and the men adjourn for a drink. In August, 1914, every novelist was angry with the war; he would rather have the little groups of casual acquaintances talking excitedly about the one thing most important to him. Even in the absence of journalistic sensations, life is always the ruthless enemy of art; the novelist fears the bridge party, the dramatist fears the oysters and champagne. So the teacher fears the football game which is imminent, and the fiery preacher

the soggy Sunday dinner, which will stupefy
the audience he has momentarily awakened to
a sense of spiritual values. Art loses much in
a vicious circle; the singers cannot be supported without the boxes, and the boxes do not
always respond to the singer's soul, and they
are often empty during the early and during
the late portions of the great opera. The faithful gallery has the thrills, but lacks the cash.
The West End dramatist is the one who reaps
the harvest of gold; and his plays are supported
by grown-up children and must be modelled to
their necessities. For although God never
tempers the wind to the shorn lamb, the artist
finds it expedient to do so. The novelist may
aim his work at the highest intelligence; but the
highest intelligence borrows or reads the book
in a public library, adding nothing to the
author's royalties. If it is to make an immediate fortune for him, he must perhaps com-
promise with his soul. If it is to be published
in a limited and beautiful edition, it will be
owned by those who will never cut the leaves.
The greatest portrait painter cannot always

select interesting faces; he is doomed to paint those who have his price.

This fear of indifference, frivolity, lack of response on the part of those by whom the work of art is made possible has afflicted many a creative genius.   At the very beginning of *Père Goriot* Balzac roared in his reader's face: "This drama is neither fiction nor romance. It is so true that each one can recognise its elements in his own home; yes, perchance in his own heart."

Everything works together for evil against art. The only possible salvation is sincerity. The duration and depth of the impression made by a realistic novel are both in direct proportion to its approximation to reality; whether the reality be in the events, in the characters, or in both.

CHAPTER II

THE AGE OF ANNE

Modern realism in the age of Anne—modern English prose style—the parents of the English novel—Daniel Defoe and his realistic romances—the style of *Gulliver's Travels*—the three ways of telling a story—Richardson and the psychological novel.

THE men of Queen Anne brought prose fiction from heaven or hell to earth, and gave us the novel. Of all centuries, the eighteenth holds the primacy as the Century of Beginnings; and perhaps for this reason we of the twentieth have a higher regard for it than the Victorians expressed. During the fifteen years of the present epoch, there has been a noticeable rehabilitation of the eighteenth century; so that it already seems strange to remember that sixty years ago "the age of prose and reason" stood low in public esteem. We know now that the English Augustans, with all their limitations, had a sense of fact that is worth having. Their world was a real world, and they made the best of it. Its pleasures were real, its pains were real; and when they spoke of the comforts and social delights of urban life, they knew exactly what they were talking about. They were like the Parisians; in all spheres of art, they rated cerebration higher than passion. They hated mystery and enthusiasm as being somehow symptomatic of a sloven and unkempt mind; they loved clarity, regularity, and the restraint that accompanies good breeding. The reaction against the Puritan religious excesses of the imagination was still powerful; and the wearisome sectarian controversies of the seventeenth century had developed a kind of polite scepticism, which took the shape of a general conformity to the Church of England. This earth was good enough, without supersensual speculation; and the best thing in this earth was London. They took the cash, and let the credit go.

One reason why Queen Anne literature is so clear is because it isn't deep. Writers avoided difficult themes, and confined themselves to subjects entirely within the range of limited minds.

These men were all realists, whether they wrote
verse or prose—Addison, Swift, Pope, Steele,
Defoe, Prior, Gay, Parnell, Arbuthnot—they
looked down and not up. It was an age of
criticism; and while it is not always true that
poetry is a criticism of life, the novel most certainly is. It was by no accident that the novel
was born at that time. Those intensely modern, sophisticated, clear-headed folk, with a
dominant sense of fact, had precisely the right
equipment to produce realistic fiction. This
is shown by the astounding result—the first
three English novelists will rank for all time
in the highest class. In the English novel there
is no early development from crudity to perfection, from simple to complex; the thing began
with an immortal masterpiece.

The history of literature is full of paradoxes.
English literature is instinctively and primarily romantic, as French literature is not. Yet
every attempt of the English—from *Morte
d'Arthur* in 1485 to *Waverley* in 1814—to produce a prose romance, was an ignominious failure. It is an extraordinary fact, that with the

single and glorious exception of Malory's *Morte d'Arthur,* there is not one work of prose fiction in English up to the time of Defoe that is worth the time and attention of the general reader. For I certainly would not read, nor advise any one to read *Euphues, Arcadia, Rosalind, Jack Wilton,* or *Oroonoko,* for their intrinsic value. The fact that most of those works were once "best sellers" has not saved them; they live now only in their historical significance.

The novel, next to the realistic play, is the most concrete and "natural" form of literature; and it did not appear until there was an adequate medium of expression. A simple, flexible, smooth-running English prose style did not exist until the latter half of the seventeenth century. The first person who had the knack of writing conversationally—that is, writing in a manner that reminds one of the speech of human beings—was the professional poet, Abraham Cowley. He wrote prose with his left hand; but he was left-handed. Cowley was a born prosateur, as his poetry proves. His pretentious odes are like sign-posts pointing

in the direction of poetry, which do not move
themselves. His cumbersome, nickel-plated
epic, *Davideis,* seems like Saul's huge armour,
with David rattling around inside of it. But
the prose parts of his essays, which he wrote
just to please himself, have all the charm of
the conversation of a cultivated gentleman.
The great Dryden went to school to Cowley;
and although he acknowledged again and again
his debt to his teacher's verse, he really owed
more to the prose. No writer who ever lived
was more a man of his own age than John
Dryden; and he seems to have perceived that
Cowley had a command of a truly natural and
essentially modern prose style. What is meant
by this will be immediately apparent by comparing a passage from Milton with a passage
from Cowley.

From the *Areopagitica:*

Methinks I see in my mind a noble and puissant
nation rousing herself like a strong man after sleep,
and shaking her invincible locks: methinks I see her
as an eagle mewing her mighty youth, and kindling
her undazzled eyes at the full midday beam; purging

and unscaling her long abused sight at the fountain
itself of heavenly radiance, while the whole noise of
timorous and flocking birds, with those that love
the twilight, flutter about, amazed at what she means,
and in their envious gabble would prognosticate a
year of sects and schisms.

From *A Discourse Concerning the Govern-
ment of Oliver Cromwell:*

It was the funeral day of the late man who made
himself to be called protector. And though I bore
but little affection, either to the memory of him, or
to the trouble and folly of all public pageantry, yet
I was forced by the importunity of my company to
go along with them, and be a spectator of that solem-
nity, the expectation of which had been so great that
it was said to have brought some very curious persons (and no doubt singular virtuosos) as far as from
the Mount in Cornwall, and from the Orcades. I
found there had been much more cost bestowed than
either the dead man, or indeed death itself, could
deserve. . . . The vast multitude of spectators made
up, as it uses to do, no small part of the spectacle itself. But yet, I know not how, the whole was so
managed that, methought, it somewhat represented
the life of him for whom it was made; much noise,
much tumult, much expense, much magnificence, much
vainglory; briefly, a great show, and yet, after all
this, but an ill sight.

Dryden, with his love of what was rational and unaffected, seems to have adopted Cowley's method of prose composition, and carried it to perfection. Dryden is called the Father of English prose: he left to his successors a prose style that combined simplicity, ease, and distinction; a model followed immediately by Defoe, Swift, Addison and Steele.

The English novel of manners had for its parents the Character Books and the Periodical Essay. With the decay of the Elizabethan Drama, the Character Books became popular. They were collections of sketches of familiar types of people; the object of the writer being to give in as small as possible space a complete pen-picture of A Scholar, A Courtier, A Milkmaid, A Soldier, or whatever representative of humanity he happened to select. Although this species of literature was ostensibly objective, it was really self-conscious to the last degree. The author put his own personality into each sketch, filling in the outline with pungent comment. These character books helped to satisfy the natural curiosity of readers about human nature, especially after the opportunity to see human nature reveal itself on the stage was gone. A particular group of persons was isolated, and its main characteristics sharply emphasised; an undercurrent of satire salting the sketch. Thus it was natural that Samuel Butler, the famous author of *Hudibras,* should have been a prominent contributor to this school; although the most successful member of it was Bishop John Earle, who, in his *Microcosmographie* (1628) produced a portfolio of university portraits many of which would even to-day be recognised instantly as faithful likenesses. The Character Books flourished in the seventeenth century, and furnished all the material for a realistic novel except the fable.

This was supplied by the periodical essay, which reached fruition in the *Spectator* (1711), where the manners and customs of the day were accurately reflected. Here the Character Sketch ceased to be static, as in the Character Books, and became dynamic. It was just the difference between the photograph and the moving picture. A person or group of persons was picked up, and carried along through certain familiar experiences. This method reached its climax in the popular Sir Roger de Coverley papers, where, in portraying the varied activities of this charming gentleman in town and country, the author was forced into actual narrative, which just misses being a connected story with a formal plot.

Thus, with the sharp isolation of character, singled out, plainly labelled, a pin stuck through it to fix it in place, and then microscopically analysed—together with narrative sketches of contemporary scenes in town and country life, we have the two parents from whom our modern realistic fiction came.

Although Defoe certainly wrote the first English novel, there was a story published in 1680, that differs from a genuine realistic novel only in intention. This was *The Life and Death of Mr. Badman,* by John Bunyan. It is a faithful picture of a contemporary man in a contemporary environment; a history of the times and manners related in a downright, straightforward style; and the restraint in the account

of the death-scene shows exquisite art. The
author wrote the book as a religious tract;
otherwise it might rank as the earliest novel in
the English language.

The first English novel is still one of the most
popular—*Robinson Crusoe*, by Daniel Defoe,
published in 1719. Defoe was fifty-eight years
old when he wrote this story; and he had been
scribbling steadily for over thirty years. He
was a consummate realist, with a keen sense of
fact; he had a telescopic imagination, and a
microscopic eye. In subject-matter, *Robinson
Crusoe* is wildly romantic; in method and in
style, it is studiously realistic. For even in his
romances, Defoe had the realistic manner, just
as Victor Hugo in his realistic novels had the
romantic style. Defoe describes life on a remote island as George Gissing would describe
a London street; Victor Hugo writes of the
sewers of Paris with superbly picturesque eloquence. Defoe's genius for detail is what has
made his masterpiece such a hot favourite with
boys; the matter-of-fact boy never thinks to
ask, Is it true? because he knows it is true,

every page of it. Boys are immediately tied to
the wheels of his narrative, and follow like
slaves.

The enormous popularity of *Robinson Crusoe* has buried its author's name and overshad-
owed all his other works of fiction; I suspect
that not merely boys, but many men and women
of some culture, would find it easier to give
the name of Robinson's servant than that of
his creator; and how many general readers
know *Moll Flanders* and *Captain Singleton?*
I remember a good talk on books I enjoyed once
with a distinguished Boston physician, who,
though he had been brought up on *Robinson
Crusoe,* did not know the name Defoe, and did
not suspect that the author of *Crusoe* had written other novels. He was much interested, and
carefully wrote down the titles for subsequent
perusal. Yet it is true that if Defoe had never
written his island story, he would still rank as
the first English novelist, and as a realistic
author of genius. For *Moll Flanders* (1722)
and *Roxana* (1724) are shining examples of absolute realism; they are, in the strictest use of

the word, as truly realistic novels as is *Jonathan Wild* (1743) or *Mrs. Martin's Man* (1914).
They give accurate pictures of the slums, with
plans and specifications.

Even in his story of sheer imagination, dealing with a region as remote from Defoe's experience as Paradise, the author sticks faithfully to the realistic method. In *Captain
Singleton* (1720) Defoe took his readers across
the Dark Continent. The book is filled with
amazingly good guesses, many of which have
been verified by explorers; and although, to
those who really know the interior of Africa,
the Captain's experiences might often arouse
laughter, the whole thing sounds convincing
enough to the tenderfoot. To me indeed it
seems more truthful, and perhaps is, than the
majority of "books of travel" I have read.
For Defoe was a skilful and an artistic liar,
who had considerable respect for his audience;
whereas many travellers and explorers seem to
under-estimate the intelligence and overrate the
receptivity of those who stay at home. I suspect that this book had a greater influence on

Stevenson than any other of Defoe's: we know from the former's statement that he studied the literary style of the first novelist with assiduity. To test the result, I read through *Captain Singleton* and immediately after read *The Master of Ballantrae;* and it was astonishing to see such extraordinary resemblance free from all taint of plagiarism.

Every historian of literature will say that Defoe came closest to actual fact in his *Journal of the Plague Year* (1722), which has constantly been cited as showing the marvellous power of his imagination. Librarians and cataloguers who have classified it as " history " have been treated by the critics with a tolerant smile, for is not such acceptation a tribute to the author's genius? It has remained for Dr. Watson Nicholson to discover and to prove that Defoe's work is not imagination, but rather the coherent assembling of facts and figures. Even in Defoe's wildest romances, he always seems to have his "sources": which, instead of being old ballads and poetic chronicles, were more like city directories, vital statistics, and cash accounts. I always used to wonder how it had been possible to describe that Plague Year with such convincing detail, when Defoe was simply sitting at his desk, spinning it all out of his imagination, and "making it up as he went along." But Dr. Nicholson has studied the originals, and the comparison shows that Defoe stuck adhesively to his facts. Thus the famous *Journal* is history, after all, and not fiction; only it is history narrated by a great artist.

For of all the works of Defoe, the *Journal of the Plague Year* shows the most complete mastery of prose style. The following passage is a proof that this author could occasionally bring off the rarest of all accomplishments in any form of art—he could make the finished result an absolute realisation of his intention.

A certain citizen, who had lived safe and untouched till the month of September, when the weight of the distemper lay more in the city than it had done before, was mighty cheerful, and something too bold, as I think it was, in his talk of how secure he was, how cautious he had been, and how he had never come near any sick body. Says another citizen, a neighbour of his, to him one day, "Do not be too confident, Mr. ——, it is hard to say who is sick and who is well; for we see men alive and well, to outward appearance, one hour, and dead the next." "That is true," says the first man, for he was not a man presumptuously secure, but had escaped a long while; and men, as I said above, especially in the City, began to be over easy upon that score. "That is true," says he, "I do not think myself secure, but I hope I have not been in company with any person that there has been any danger in." "No!" says his neighbour, "was not you at the Bull-head tavern, in Gracechurch Street, with Mr. ——, the night before last?" "Yes," says the first, "I was, but there was nobody there that we had any reason to think dangerous." Upon which his neighbour said no more, being unwilling to surprise him; but this made him more inquisitive, and as his neighbour appeared backward, he was the more impatient, and in a kind of warmth, says he aloud, "Why, he is not dead, is he?" Upon which his neighbour still was silent, but cast up his eyes, and said something to himself; at which the first citizen turned pale, and said no more but this, "Then I am a dead man too," and went home immediately, and sent for a neighbouring apothecary to give him something preventive, for he had not yet found himself ill; but the apothecary opening his breast, fetched a sigh, and said no more but this, "Look up to God"; and the man died in a few hours.

Never was there a better illustration of the superiority of concrete instance over abstract statement and general description. The above paragraph gives a clearer impression of the ravages of the plague than long chapters of rhetorical emphasis could have done. If only preachers and philosophers would sit at the feet of Defoe! Compare *The Varieties of Religious Experience* in interest (and in importance) with the majority of works on metaphysics.

Our first English novelist set a notable example to his followers, in objectivity. Neither Flaubert nor his disciple Guy de Maupassant succeeded in holding themselves more aloof from their characters than did Defoe. It is amusing to remember that he called *Robinson Crusoe* an allegory and pretended that his slum stories had an ethical basis; if we had only his novels, we should know no more about his character and opinions than we know of William Shakespeare.

A work that surely owed something to *Robinson Crusoe,* though emanating from a far greater mind, was *Gulliver's Travels* (1726).

This is probably the best-written work of fiction in the English language, for there has never lived a writer who had a more absolute command of prose than Jonathan Swift. He wrote with such astonishing ease and perfection, that it seems as if even his most secret thoughts and meditations must have taken a correct literary form. It was a fine compliment to the new art of the novel that the greatest genius of the age should have selected that form for his satire against the animal called man. This work of candid pessimism and bitter cynicism stands next to *Robinson Crusoe* as a juvenile favourite; because its marvellous imagination is made vivid by the same realism in details, and the drawings in the first two books are exactly according to scale. It is impossible to doubt either the veracity or the accuracy of the traveller. Both Bunyan and Swift would be included in the highest rank of English novelists, if their purpose in writing had not been so far afield.

Defoe was fifty-eight when he wrote *Robinson Crusoe,* Swift was fifty-nine when he wrote *Gulliver,* and Richardson was fifty-one when he

wrote *Pamela*. Possibly one reason why the
earliest forms of the English novel were so
superbly developed—for the paradox is a truth
—is because their makers were themselves so
mature. The novel, which is a critical analysis
of life, has usually been successful only when
it has been the fruit of experience, and when
the author has learned the technique of style
in other forms of composition. Of our greatest
English novelists, only one—Dickens—published a good novel before the age of thirty.

Professor Raleigh, in his admirable little
book *The English Novel*—which combines the
terse condensation of a manual with the easy
and luminous style of good armchair talk—
calls attention to the three modes of novel composition. The author may tell his story as an
invisible and omnipresent mind reader, he may
put the whole thing into the speech of the leading character, or he may depend exclusively on
epistolary correspondence. One might add that
many authors employ all three in one; the story
is told by the novelist, with the introduction of
much conversation, varied by occasional letters.

The first method is not the best for youthful readers; for they must ask, as I used to ask on reading a sentence like "Geoffrey was thinking deeply of a new plan of escape,"—how does the author know what Geoffrey is thinking about? Telling the story in the first person, as in *Lorna Doone* and *David Copperfield,* restricts the range while heightening vividness; the great difficulty being that we know the narrator bears a charmed life. John Ridd is sure to emerge successfully from the most unpromising situations; and the reader has more curiosity than suspense. Professor Moulton says that many people read novels with only a sporting interest, to see how the books end; this method should dull their attention. Dickens evidently felt the danger of this system, for the first sentence in *David Copperfield* reads, "Whether I shall turn out to be the hero of my own life, or whether that station will be held by anybody else, these pages must show." In *Treasure Island* Stevenson really solved the problem; he obtained all the advantages of this method with none of its drawbacks; for the story is told in

the first person, but by one of the least important characters. Thus we have constant vividness, with no sense of security. The third way,
having the whole novel consist of letters, is valuable only for mature readers; but perhaps it
is the best for revelation of character in its most
elemental passions and most trivial caprices.
Perhaps it is also best for creating and main-
taining the illusion. In a way, too, this plan
combines the excellences of the second and third
methods. When a story is told in the first
person, it is like reading a long letter from one
character, as the first paragraph of any such
novel will prove; in a series of letters by different hands, one gains all the vitality of direct discourse, with the advantages of a varied company, any one of whom may meet a tragic end.

It is rather interesting to remember that our
first three professional novelists adopted in
their respective masterpieces the three different
styles of fiction. Defoe had Robinson Crusoe
tell his own story; Richardson developed the
character of Clarissa in a series of letters; and
Fielding wrote the "history" of Tom Jones.

We have here an interesting comparison of three
great artists at work. I suppose that if most
critics were asked to state a preference, they
would say, "The greatest of these is Fielding."
If they were asked to name the least didactic,
once more they would say Fielding. Yet I believe that the art of Defoe and Richardson has
more aloofness, more objectivity, more severity
and more sincerity than the art of Fielding; and
that however anxious Defoe and Richardson
may have been to strengthen the forces of conventional morality, however "preachy" they
may have been by nature, their two masterpieces
are distinctly less didactic than *Tom Jones*.
For the method according to which *Robinson*
and *Clarissa* were written forbade the intrusion
of the author; whereas Fielding, by adopting
the scheme most popular among his successors,
gave himself full liberty to interpose in the
story, to comment on its progress, on the characters, on life in general; in doing this, he established a bad precedent in English fiction; for
English novelists have been notable for didactic
and sentimental interruptions in their narra-

tives, and for a condescending attitude toward
their readers; both of which habits aid in de-
stroying the illusion and lead to downright insincerity.

Enormous is the difference between Richardson's prefaces and Richardson's novels. His
prefaces are like the rhetorical and tedious pre-
liminary remarks delivered by the lecturer while
the lights are on; and we begin the first chapter
with the same relief and expectancy that the
audience greet the extinction of the lamps and
the language, and see the snow-capped mountain
leap into view. For however the orator may
rave and moralise about the mountain, the
mountain itself is objective. The moment Richardson leaves his damnable faces and begins,
he is an absolute artist. No novel that I can
think of has a more direct opening than *Pamela;*
the attention of the reader is instantly captured;
and in the first paragraph both the heroine and
villain are presented. At the end of the preface, Richardson withdraws from the story —
even as the alloy left Browning's famous ring
with one spirt of the acid. If we did not know

the greatness of Richardson the novelist, Richardson the preacher would block the way. Let us compare the opening sentences of the preface to *Pamela* with the first words of the novel.

If to Divert and Entertain, *and at the same time to Instruct and* Improve *the Minds of the* YOUTH *of* both Sexes:

If to inculcate Religion *and* Morality *in so easy and agreeable a manner, as shall render them equally* delightful *and* profitable:

If to set forth in the most exemplary Lights, the Parental, *the* Filial, *and the* Social *Duties:*

(All this is followed by seven other ifs.)

We turn to the first page of the story.

Dear Father and Mother,—I have great trouble, and some comfort, to acquaint you with. The trouble is, that my good lady died of the illness I mentioned to you, and left us all much grieved for the loss of her; for she was a dear good lady, and kind to all us her servants. Much I feared, that as I was taken by her ladyship to wait upon her person, I should be quite destitute again, and forced to return to you and my poor mother, who have enough to do to maintain yourselves; and, as my lady's goodness had put me to write and cast accounts, and made me a little expert at my needle, and otherwise qualified above my degree, it was not every family that could have found a place that your poor Pamela was fit for: but God, whose graciousness to us we have so often experienced at a pinch, put it into my good lady's heart on her death-bed, just an hour before she expired, to recommend to my young master all her servants, one by one; and when it came to my turn to be recommended (for I was sobbing and crying at her pillow), she could only say, My dear son!—and so broke off a little; and then recovering—Remember my poor Pamela— And these were some of her last words! Oh, how my eyes run—don't wonder to see the paper so blotted.

After another paragraph, she signs the letter, and then adds a postscript:

I have been scared out of my senses; for just now, as I was folding up this letter in my late lady's dressing-room, in comes my young master! Good sirs! how was I frightened! I went to hide the letter in my bosom; and he, seeing me tremble, said, smiling, "To whom have you been writing, Pamela?" etc.

Richardson felt the necessity of writing apologies for his great works of fiction. But his apologies are written in a cramped and intolerably formal style, full of canting generalities. The instant he begins his story, it is as though he threw off a mask, resumed his natural voice, and narrated without any didactic ardour. For the letters in the story seldom begin with generalities, but are intensely concrete and intensely dramatic. The difference between the tone of the prefaces and the tone of the story is like the change in many a parson's voice when he has finished the grace before meat, and begins to talk about the weather.

The immense length of Richardson's novels is part of his scheme, and yet he does remind us of the after-dinner speaker who was pleasantly introduced by the toastmaster as an orator of excellent initiative, but totally lacking in terminal facilities. I sometimes think that his novels were not meant to be read by individuals but by dynasties and generations; the grandfather puts in a bookmark and dies, and his mature son takes up the burden at that point. Yet the proof that Richardson was correct in his proportions is seen in the fact that every attempt to abridge his novels has been a failure. Much better never to read *Clarissa* than to read it clipped. Its length is an essential feature of the plot. Richardson had the genius for expansion shown by Robert Browning in the *Ring and*

the Book; there is more than one close analogy
between *Clarissa* and that epic. The whole
story can be told in a dozen lines; but in each
case the author has expanded it into volumes.
There is not now any interest of suspense; the
poet gave the whole plot away at the start, and
every modern reader knows what happened to
Clarissa. The object of the artist in each case
was complete psychological analysis; which
could not have been achieved except by accumulation of detail. Richardson is the originator
of the psychological novel; and in two respects
he has never been surpassed—in the tireless patience of his analysis, and in his unflinching
march toward the inevitable tragic close.

CHAPTER III

FIELDING, SMOLLETT, STERNE

Popularity and immortality—the reason why Richardson's Continental fame exceeded Fielding's—effect of the personal essay—the insincerity of Fielding—its bad influence on the English novel—Fielding's didacticism—his humour—comic men and tragic women—sensational titles to novels—Smollett the naturalist—Dr. Johnson and Rasselas —Goldsmith—the personality of Sterne—the sentimental novel in the eighteenth century—the sentimental novel in the twentieth century.

IT is a common and pathetic delusion of unpopular writers to believe that at their death their works will not follow them, but will remain to charm "millions yet unborn." Unfortunately for this faith, which has been the solace and the stimulus of many fictionists, the fact is that there has never been a great English novelist who was not popular in his own lifetime. The world often runs after false gods, but it seldom neglects true deities. What revealing element is there in true works of genius that makes their transcendent merit so instantly manifest to thousands of uncultivated people? Sometimes it seems as if the greatness of a literary work were as unmistakable—as immediately clear— as the size of a tall man. An astronomer knows more about stars than the man in the street; but the superior brilliance of a star of the first magnitude is as evident to the untrained eyes as to the expert. When the object judged is really important, future generations do little more than ratify contemporary opinion. No one has ever improved on Ben Jonson's criticism of Shakespeare, of Dryden's appraisal of Milton. Defoe, Swift, and Richardson were as much admired by their contemporaries, and for precisely the same reasons, as they are praised to-day.

The London success of *Pamela* and *Clarissa* is therefore not in the least surprising; but it is rather remarkable that they should have aroused such ecstatic wonder among the French, that they should have thrilled three men so different as Diderot, the Abbé Prévost and Rousseau, and should have proved to be an actual

contributory force to the French Revolution.
One reason why Richardson was so much more
popular on the Continent than Fielding, was because Richardson lost nothing in translation;
Fielding lost irreparably. You can translate a
story; you cannot translate a style. For the
same reason, Cooper has been a hundred times
more widely read in Europe than Hawthorne;
the wonderful grace, distinction, and shy aus-
terity of Hawthorne's language vanish in a
translation; whereas every time you translate
Cooper, you improve him. He was a marvellous romancer, with a good story, fascinating
characters, and bad style; so that I have always believed that the French, the Germans, the
Poles, the Russians really have a finer collec-
tion of Leather-Stocking Tales than the Americans.

Fielding, like his disciple Thackeray, was a
natural-born humourist, with a sure instinct for
burlesque. To him Richardson was as intolerable as were the Puritans to the Cavaliers. For
over ten years Fielding had been having a merry
time with stage burlesque when *Pamela* ap-

peared; its prodigious success aroused every fibre of opposition in his soul, for to him it represented smug, canting hypocrisy—the religion of the scribes and Pharisees. We may rejoice that it stung him into creative composition; although he was of course constitutionally incapable of appreciating either Richardson's artistic merits or his immense significance.

Although the Character Book and the Periodical Essay were the parents of the English novel, a third species of literature seems to have had a powerful influence on Fielding, and still more on Fielding's successor, Sterne. This was the Personal Essay, a peculiarly individual kind of writing, totally different from critical essays like Matthew Arnold's and from reflective essays on abstract themes, like Bacon's or Emerson's. It is an intimate, confessional style of composition, where the writer takes the reader completely into his confidence, and talks as if to only one listener; talks, too, about things often essentially trivial, and yet making them for the moment interesting by the charm of the speaker's manner. The first great master of this school remains supreme and unapproachable—Montaigne, a universal favourite with lovers of books. Burton's *Anatomy of Melancholy* is a kind of monstrous personal essay; the species was immortally illustrated in the seventeenth century by Cowley, by Browne in the whimsical and fantastic *Garden of Cyrus,* by Tom Fuller in *Good Thoughts in Bad Times;* and some of the papers in the *Tatler, Spectator,* and *Guardian* could be classed in this group. No literature we have is more self-conscious than this; and of all eighteenth-century novelists, none was more self-conscious than Henry Fielding.

In his first novel, *Joseph Andrews* (1742), he was not content with writing a general and (to me) rather tedious introduction to the whole work; three of the four books into which the story is divided are respectively introduced with a short personal essay. This custom was continued in *Tom Jones;* and however charming, witty, and satirical they may be, they break the continuity of the narrative, destroy the illusion, and disconcert the reader; it is as if, before each

act of a great comedy, the author should appear
before the footlights, and condescendingly address the audience.

It may seem odd to accuse Fielding of anything like insincerity; and yet these side talks
with his readers, these constant intrusions of
the master of the show, are not only funda-
mentally insincere from the point of view of
art, they established a bad tradition in English
fiction. Far too many of our British novelists
have regarded themselves as caterers, whose
business is to tickle the palate of the reading
public; and they have followed in the wake of
Fielding. In the first chapter of the second
book of *Joseph Andrews,* we read, "It becomes
an author generally to divide a book, as it does
a butcher to joint his meat, for such assistance
is of great help to both the reader and the
carver. And now, having indulged myself a
little, I will endeavour to indulge the curiosity
of my reader, who is no doubt impatient to
know what he will find in the subsequent chapters of this book."

This attitude toward the reader was faith-

fully followed by many Anglo-Saxon novelists;
many instances could be given; but one of the
best echoes of Fielding's personal remarks may
be found in the second chapter of Anthony
Trollope's *Doctor Thorne*: "A few words must
still be said about Miss Mary before we rush
into our story; the crust will then have been
broken, and the pie will be open to the guests."
The difference between sincerity in Russian fiction and in English fiction may be expressed
by saying that in *Tom Jones* we admire the
carefully planned and well executed realism;
in *Anna Karenina* we are in a world of absolute
reality.

It is often said by critics who should know
better that Richardson was not only offensively
didactic, but that his view of morality was low;
because he emphasises the *rewards* of a moral
life, either in substantial worldly advantages
or in sorrowless immortality; whereas Fielding
was never consciously didactic, and represented
the dividends of virtue simply in increased
greatness of character. To settle the truth of
these statements, let us read what Richardson

wrote to Lady Bradshaigh, who was not satisfied to have Clarissa get her reward in heaven, but preferred a little earthly felicity. The author wrote, "Clarissa has the greatest of triumphs even in this world. The greatest, I will venture to say, even in and after the outrage, and because of the outrage, that ever woman had."

And in reply to the statement that Fielding is not consciously didactic, but is willing to let the moral of his books speak for itself, we have simply to read the first paragraph of the dedication of *Amelia*: "The following book is sincerely designed to promote the cause of virtue, and to expose some of the most glaring evils, as well public as private, which at present infest the country."

Fielding speaks more persuasively as a great humourist; one of the greatest in English literature. His view of the world had the immense tolerance and profound sympathy of the true humourist, along with keenness of observation whetted by satire. The ground quality of his mind was humour. In *Joseph An-*

drews it took the form of burlesque; intended originally as a parody on Richardson and Colley Cibber, it widened into a broad creative work, retaining the burlesque element in the scenes of rough farce. In *Jonathan Wild* it took the form of irony, irony on a vast, universal scale. In *Tom Jones,* his masterpiece, it supplied exactly the right medium in which all the characters lived, and moved, and had their being, besides enabling him to give that wonderful type-portrait of Squire Western. In *Amelia,* it furnished that deep tenderness inevitably characteristic of great humourists.

The never-drying springs of humour in Fielding's nature gave a richness, fruitiness, variety, and complexity to his novels that one misses in Richardson; and yet, had the author of *Clarissa* possessed a sense of humour, he could not possibly have written a work of such detailed, profound, and prolonged analysis. His mind would have reacted on itself, and he would have looked upon his own creations ironically, as Fielding did. Furthermore, Fielding was essentially a comic writer, and Richardson at his best in tragedy. Once more, Richardson was more successful in depicting women than men; Fielding just the contrary. Mr. B— and Sir Charles do not compare for a moment with Parson Adams, Tom Jones, and Squire Western; but neither will Sophia or Amelia live for a moment when placed beside Pamela and Clarissa. Now it is impossible to draw the character of a man convincingly without a sense of humour; whereas in the portrayal of a perfectly natural woman this quality is not necessary. Say what you will about the equality of the sexes, man is essentially a comic character; and woman, tragic.

Fielding's men are wonderful—being, like all real men, imperfectly tamed beasts. Thomas Gray, an inveterate reader of French novels, was advised by his friend, Richard West, to read the new story *Joseph Andrews,* and his criticism after doing so remains true unto this day. "The incidents are ill laid and without invention; but the characters have a great deal of nature, which always pleases even in her lowest shapes. Parson Adams is perfectly well; so is Mrs. Slipslop, and the story of Wilson; and throughout he shows himself well read in Stage-Coaches, Country Squires, Inns, and Inns of Court. His reflections upon high people and low people, and misses and masters, are very good. However the exaltedness of some minds (or rather as I shrewdly suspect their insipidity and want of feeling or observation) may make them insensible to these light things (I mean such as characterise and paint nature), yet surely they are as weighty and much more useful than your grave discourses upon the mind, the passions, and what not."

Thomas Gray combined profound scholarship with a hatred of pedantry; the fact that his fastidious mind recognised immediately the artistic dignity of a truthful portrayal of low life, is one more example of the hospitality of his soul. And this first criticism of *Joseph Andrews* convicts of shallowness persons who read works on philosophy and metaphysics, and scorn novels; for a great novel is simply a profound study in the concrete of what philosophy attempts in the abstract. The "exaltedness" of some minds, is, as Gray says, often a mask which conceals a "want of feeling or observation."

The real defect in *Joseph Andrews* was pointed out immediately by Gray, just as he saw its greatest virtue. The incidents would have been better managed had not the author started with the avowed intention of composing a burlesque; this blemish in Fielding's first novel is conspicuously absent in *Tom Jones,* which, according to Coleridge, has one of the three greatest plots in all literature. In *Joseph Andrews,* the basis of the novel is not a story; in *Tom Jones,* it is. Fielding became a master workman; and handled the intricacies of this orderly narrative with impressive ease.

Ambitious authors who hunt for sensational titles to attract the public would do well to remember that the majority of immortal novels have common-place names. In Fielding's masterpiece the name is intentionally commonplace, for it might equally as well have been called the History of a Man. Thackeray's remark about it is not really true, and if it were, it would not reflect much credit on Thackeray.

Tom Jones is meant to be a memorandum rather than a model.   He is not what we ought to become, but what too many of us are; and the real reason why men and women are so fond of him is because he is a perfectly healthy male; as Mrs. Atherton would say, he is one hundred per cent. masculine.

With environment altered, Tom Jones would be a faithful portrait in the twentieth century; Sophia Western would not do at all.

Coarseness and fineness are the characteristics respectively of the work of Smollett and Sterne.   One used an axe, the other a needle. Richardson was an analyst, Fielding a realist, Smollett a naturalist.   Smollett was not by nature a creative artist, as Fielding undoubtedly was; he was a man of fact rather than fancy; and his experiences gave him more material than inspiration.   He was a physician and a sailor; he broke into the ranks of the novelists by brute force, and has retained his position by the same quality.   He wrote stories, where the travelling hero wanders rather aimlessly through a series of adventures.   An excellent illustration of this kind of novel is seen in 1915 in Sinclair Lewis's *The Trail of the Hawk*.

His first two novels are exactly contemporary with the masterpieces of Richardson and Fielding; for *Roderick Random* appeared in 1748, and *Peregrine Pickle* in 1751. The immense vitality of these two novels won a sure place both in contemporary favour and in the history of literature; outweighing glaring faults in construction, and many crudities and excrescences. The indecencies of his books were patent to every one except the author, who said, in the third edition of *Peregrine Pickle,* "He flatters himself that he has expunged every adventure, phrase, and insinuation, that could be construed by the most delicate reader into a trespass upon the rules of decorum." Writers are the worst judges in the world of the morality of their works; he writeth, and wipeth his pen, and saith, "I have done no wickedness."

Richardson declared, in the preface to *Pamela,* that he had composed the work "without raising a single idea throughout the whole, that shall shock the exactest purity, even in the warmest of those instances where purity would be most apprehensive." When Vanbrugh was attacked by Jeremy Collier he said he had never written anything that the most virtuous damsel might not keep in her chamber with her Bible. Perhaps no man is ever quite so absurd as when he is defending himself from a just accusation.

Smollett is a man's novelist; I have never heard a woman praise him. There is no doubt that men enjoy buffoonery, horse-play, and rough farce; women not only do not enjoy these things, they cannot understand how or why refined and educated men should enjoy them. Mrs. Oliphant could not comprehend the general praise of Burns's *Jolly Beggars;* and after fruitless speculation, she finally reached the wise conclusion that the difference in her appreciation was simply a difference of sex. "There must always be, we presume, however age and experience may modify nature, a certain inability on the part of a woman to appreciate the more riotous forms of mirth, and that robust freedom in morals which bolder minds admire. It is a disability which nothing can abolish.''

Men often laugh at women for their interest in what seems to men trivialities, details of clothing, ''social columns'' and ''woman's page'' in the newspapers; but women find it incomprehensible that a great scholar like Burton should delight in the coarse repartee of the bargemen, and that cultivated gentlemen should read with close attention two columns of fine print, consisting of statements like this: ''At the beginning of the fifth round, Jack ducked, and delivered a jolt in the slats.''

I once met a United States Army lieutenant, a gentleman of wide reading and good taste, who told me without the slightest doubt the greatest novel in the English language was *Humphry Clinker*. Smollett wrote it while he was dying, and it is notable that this robust and healthy masterpiece should come from a mortally sick man, though a hundred years later another and greater Scot brought the same event to pass. Smollett followed the scheme of Richardson in this novel, putting it into the form of letters, its only resemblance to his predecessor. This book is full of rich coarse humour, and has at the same time the preserving quality of original genius.

To read Smollett's novels is like witnessing, from a safe coign of vantage, a free fight, hearing resounding whacks and resounding oaths. For Smollett's heroes do not talk as if they had been no further than Finsbury; much of his humour consists in his language. Why is it that every one in the audience laughs when the man on the stage says "damn"?

Critics whose zeal for parallels exceeds their knowledge of the subject, have often repeated the saying that Thackeray is the child of Fielding, and Dickens of Smollett. The considerable amount of truth in the first half of the statement should not lead to any acceptance of the second. No two novelists in English literature are more unlike than Smollett and Dickens. Of all our writers of fiction, Smollett is the most heartless; he had a gusto for life, and men and women amused him prodigiously; but his books show no tenderness and no real sympathy, for

if he had possessed these qualities, his work
would have been more complex. Balzac wrote
the human comedy: Smollett wrote the human
farce. Now the one absolutely dominating
characteristic of Dickens is tenderness; he had
the mind of a man, and the heart of a child.

Again, of all British novelists—with the possible exception of Sterne—Smollett is the least
spiritual; there is no other-worldliness in *Roderick Random* or *Peregrine Pickle*. There is
not only no Christian element in these stories,
there is no religious atmosphere of any kind.
Dickens, on the other hand, is one of the most
powerful allies of Christianity that English
literature has ever produced. The whole foundation of his works is the love of God and the
love of man.

Dr. Johnson is numbered among the novelists
as Saul was among the prophets. He was not
exactly fitted to write so concrete a form of literature, and the wonder is, as he said of the
woman and the dog, that he could do it at all.
It is commonly stated (incorrectly) that he
wrote *Rasselas* (1759) to defray the expenses

of his mother's funeral; to-day, could such a work get into print, it might conceivably hasten the funeral of its author. Remembering the spirited beginning of *Pamela,* it is instructive to read the opening sentence of *Rasselas:*—

Ye who listen with credulity to the whispers of fancy, and pursue with eagerness the phantoms of hope; who expect that age will perform the promises of youth, and that the deficiencies of the present day will be supplied by the morrow;—attend to the history of Rasselas, prince of Abyssinia.

It is much easier to listen with credulity to the whispers of fancy, than it is to listen at all to the history of Rasselas. This novel remains in English literature an embalmed corpse, preserved by Johnson's great and noble name.

The Doctor's volatile friend, Oliver Goldsmith, had much better success; fiction being really his natural element. *The Vicar of Wakefield* (1766) has an immortal charm, a fadeless beauty. Goldsmith had all the qualifications that his learned contemporary lacked; a truly creative imagination, great facility in composition, the irresistible humorous tenderness so characteristic of the sons and daughters of Ireland. In literature Johnson was a super-dreadnought, Goldsmith an excursion steamer. Hundreds of thousands of happy men, women, and children have loved to travel anywhere with Goldy. So far as I know, there has been only one discontented passenger—Mark Twain, who said that any list of books for reading was a good list, so long as it did *not* contain *The Vicar of Wakefield.*

Smollett was a physician and Sterne a minister of the gospel; one trained in science, the other in sentiment. Both men died in middle life, but literature lost little by their early disappearance. Smollett had apparently given the world the very best that was in him; and Sterne would not have completed either *Tristram Shandy* or the *Sentimental Journey,* for the quintessence of those works is their incompleteness; and we have enough of both. Sterne was really an invalid, and the finest thing in his whole life, character, and career, is the marvellous courage he showed in facing his own disease. He regarded his frequent and violent hemorrhages with ironical humour. It is impossible to understand Sterne; he defies both analysis and appraisal. Professor Cross, in his admirable biography, has told us more about this man than was ever known before, giving us at the same time an accurate picture of the times. But Sterne is elusive.

Sterne's nature was passive rather than active. He might have said with Keats, "Oh, for a life of sensations rather than of thoughts!" He was a veritable Æolian harp, for the winds of passion, fancy, sentiment, mirth, and pathos to play on. In sheer invention he was weak, or lazy: there must be an exciting cause from without, either in some street spectacle, or in some book that he was reading. This external stimulus would set him off into the strangest vagaries and paradoxes. He was both irreverent and immoral; the coarse explicitness of Fielding and Smollett changed into evil suggestion, refined wickedness. Morally, we rate him below almost all other great English novelists, for, as Rostand says, "The sound of a kiss is less dangerous than the silence of a smile."

In sentiment Sterne was an epicure. His extraordinary sensitiveness to impressions made him instantly responsive, intensely aware, and as changeable as the wind. With women he was a philanderer, too self-conscious to be deeply passionate, too responsive to be constant. His books are the echoes of his reading without being dishonourably plagiaristic; Rabelais, Cervantes, Burton's *Anatomy of Melancholy,* and his immediate predecessors in England are all threaded into that crazy-quilt in literature, *Tristam Shandy.*

For my part, I find Sterne's humour much better than his pathos. Whatever he may have borrowed from other books, his humour was his own, subtle, pervading, and constantly giving the reader a sharp surprise. The quizzical mask of this fantastic parson conceals his intention until we are suddenly and palpably hit; and much of his humour remains unfathomable. For what Sterne's thoughts were when he looked in the mirror no one can guess. The epitaph of John Gay perhaps comes nearest to a soliloquy by our Yorick.

Life is a jest, and all things show it:
I thought so once, but now I know it.

The difference between the light cynicism of the epitaph written by Gay and the terrible indictment of the epitaph written by Swift is just the difference between the man who regards life as a joke, and the man who regards himself as the joke of life.

Sterne's pathos—with the possible exception of the famous starling—has always left me cold. The ass in the *Sentimental Journey* and the ass in *Tristram* arouse my respect for the writer's ingenuity; but if one will compare these instances with the brief sketch of the ass in Guy de Maupassant's *Mont Oriol,* he will see the difference between a professional sentimentalist in fine virtuoso work, and the profound sympathy of a great tragic artist. I do not see how any one can read that page in the French novel without tears.

The stream of Sentimentalism—enormously widened, deepened, and accelerated by Sterne,— rose in the first half of the eighteenth century, when Samuel Richardson created the Sentimental Novel. Shortly after the appearance of the final volume of *Clarissa,* the word "sentimental" was high in favour; so much so, that on 9 January, 1750, Lady Bradshaigh wrote directly to Richardson for a decision. "What, in your opinion, is the meaning of the word sentimental, so much in vogue amongst the polite, both in town and country?" Every one wore their hearts on their sleeves in those days, for daws to pick at; and Sterne, the real jackdaw of fiction, had no difficulty in putting his beak into the public heart. Richardson had got all Europe into tears, and those were golden days for the sentimentalists. A learned German professor said that he had wept away some of the most remarkable hours of his life, "in a sort of delicious misery"—a phrase that exactly expresses the strange happiness felt by thousands of readers at that time. Rousseau—the greatest sentimentalist in all history, and the most influential writer of the modern age—began *La Nouvelle Héloise* under the inspiration of *Clarissa;* this in turn led to *Werther* and the whole *Sturm und Drang* period in Germany.

No wonder the beginnings of the English novel are worth serious study, when we find their profound effect in such movements as the Wesleyan Revival in England, and the mighty revolution in France.

Sterne's *Sentimental Journey* was begotten by Richardson, though the grave printer would have disowned it; and a flood of sentimental fiction was let loose in England. Those who are able to wade in such lachrymose literature may read Mackenzie's *Man of Feeling* (1771). Its author was a young man, and he followed the fashion. English common-sense and English humour were both too strong to permit a long reign—or shall we say rain?—of such an element.

Although the Sentimental Novel could not long maintain its supremacy, there has never been a period of English literature when sentimental novels did not flourish. The most striking illustration of the success of the sentimental novel in England in the twentieth century is the prodigious vogue of *The Rosary,* a book written by the wife of an English clergyman. Unless I

am mistaken, over a million copies of this novel
have been sold in England and in America. It
is an admirable illustration of the school. In
America the immense circulation of the books
of Gene Stratton Porter bears positive testimony to the love of Anglo-Saxons for the Sentimental Novel. We can at any rate say of this
English and of this American author that their
works please many thousands of respectable
men and women.

CHAPTER IV

EIGHTEENTH CENTURY ROMANCES

The silence of forty years—the English romantic movement—Longsword—Horace Walpole, the faddist—Mrs.
Radcliffe and Monk Lewis—Northanger Abbey, the burlesque—difference between women in 1915 and women in
1815—Jane Austen and Booth Tarkington—climax of the
romantic movement in Walter Scott.

THE forty years that elapsed from the publication of *Humphry Clinker* (1771) to *Sense and
Sensibility* (1811) are notable for the absence
of good fiction. Not a single first-class novel
appeared. English manners were mirrored
and satirised by Frances Burney, and at the
very end of the century Maria Edgeworth
coined her Irish experiences; but both these ir-
reproachable novelists are faint in comparison
with the great geniuses of English fiction and
are growing fainter in the process of years.

One reason why no good novels were produced during this period was because the mighty
name of Richardson had drawn a host of imita-

tors in his wake; and while Richardson himself was and is splendid, imitations of him are nearly the last word in human tedium. Another and better reason is seen in the rise of the Romantic Movement, which gave to many absurd prose romances immense temporary fame, but which produced nothing of importance before Walter Scott.

For the first fifty years of the eighteenth century the classicists and the realists ruled; the words "gothic" and "romantic" were in bad odour; it was thought plebeian to be demonstrative; joyful enthusiasm and sobs of grief were alike unfashionable. Toward the close of the century any novelist of even ordinary ability could strike the once stony British heart, and streams of water flowed; everything mediæval and "gothic" became a fad; and wild tales of mystery and horror were mightily cried up.

English literature is instinctively romantic; and it took men of genius, like Pope and Swift, Richardson and Fielding, to repress and shackle the national spirit; just as in France it took a superman like Victor Hugo to fight with any success against the well-regulated and sober soul of Gallic prose. Toward the close of the eighteenth century, a natural reaction—which had begun in a variety of instinctive and unconscious ways—asserted itself against the tyranny of classicism; and as the reaction gathered force, it was guilty of absurd excesses. The eighteenth century revolt, which turned English fiction into a kind of nightmare during the last ten years, had its parallel exactly a hundred years later, in an exceedingly lively revival of romance which reached a climax in 1900.

One supremely valuable thing—that England had sought in vain for centuries—came near to being lost in all this hurly-burly; I mean a perfect English prose style. The mastery of prose, richly illustrated in fictitious narrative by Defoe, Swift, Addison, and Fielding, ceased to be characteristic of the novel—ceased to exist in the novel. Fortunately pure and natural prose was kept alive by Boswell in biography and by Gibbon in history.

Although the impatient, free spirit of Smol-

lett had found the limits of space and time
somewhat irksome, and had in *Ferdinand,
Count Fathom* sought a world at once impossible and fascinating, he can never rank as a forerunner of the romantic movement in prose fiction; for he was a realist. The first genuine
historical romance of the eighteenth century—
the first earnest of Scott's fiction—was *Longsword,* by the Rev. Thomas Leland, published
in 1762. This book to-day is unread and forgotten; but it ought to be remembered by literary
historians, for its significance is as great as its
intrinsic worth is small. In plot, story, frame-
work, setting, characterisation, this little book
is a forerunner of the great romances of Scott.
It is indeed the first modern romance of chivalry
in the English language. In the "Advertisement," the author stated that "the outlines of
the following story, and some of the incidents
and more minute circumstances, are to be found
in the ancient English historians." It is, like
Ivanhoe, a story of jousts and knightly adventures; of ladies dead and lovely knights. Ex-
alted constancy between man and maid is the

basis of the plot. The style is pneumatic, but it was the style that was to be the fashion for fifty years: dare I quote?

A youth who seemed just rising to manhood, of graceful form, tall of stature, and with limbs of perfect shape, lay sorely wounded upon the ground, languid, pale, and bloody. Over him hung one in the habit of a page [*art thou there, Truepenny?*], younger, and still more exquisitely beautiful, piercing the air with lamentations, and eagerly employed in binding up the wounds of the fallen youth with locks of comely auburn, torn from a fair though dishevelled head.

Clara Reeve was influenced by this book, and made one of the few references to it that I have been able to find. In her *Progress of Romance* (1785), the following dialogue occurs: "How is that, a Romance in the 18th century?" "Yes, a Romance in reality and not a Novel.— A story like those of the middle ages, composed of Chivalry, Love, and Religion." After some detailed discussion, the remark is made, "This work is distinguished in my list, among Novels uncommon and Original."

But it took a personage of more social prestige than the Rev. Thomas Leland to set the pace for romantic fiction. In 1764 appeared *The Castle of Otranto,* by Horace Walpole, a worthless hodge-podge of gloom and tinsel that threw England into a fever of excitement and is more responsible than any other one book for releasing the flood of tales of mystery. This is not in any real sense a forerunner of Scott, as *Longsword* was; for it is a "gothic," not a historical romance. Horace Walpole, the thoroughly sophisticated man of the world, was the last person on earth, *a priori,* who should have written this turgid stuff; but the paradox occurred simply because Walpole was a man of fashion— of fads rather than fancies—and the new romanticism was in the air. Just as a conservative person will wear flaunting and picturesque garments if they are the "latest thing," so authors and artists—whose real nature might be inclined even to cynical criticism—will sometimes be the first to scent the new movement, and start a whole pack in the hue and cry. The fact that Horace Walpole wrote *The Castle of*

Otranto is the surest evidence of the approaching reign of Romanticism.

The analogy between architecture and literature is a sound one; and as Horace Walpole had drawn the attention of London society to his "Gothic Castle" at Strawberry Hill, so now he captured them anew with his Gothic romance, written in a style that would have made Quintilian stare and gasp. It had its origin in a dream—"a very natural dream for a head like mine filled with Gothic story"—and he began to write "without knowing in the least what I intended to say or relate." In the original edition he pretended that it was a translation of an old romance that he had found, but the sudden popularity of the work caused him to acknowledge the authorship in the second printing, where his preface contains a significant statement. "It was an attempt to blend the two kinds of romance, the ancient and the modern. In the former, all was imagination and improbability; in the latter, nature is always intended to be, and sometimes has been, copied

with success. Invention has not been wanting;
but the great resources of fancy have been
dammed up, by a strict adherence to common
life.'' This last sentence shows that the romantic sentiment in art is always the same;
it is impatient of the bolts and bars of experience, unwilling to submit either to rules of
authority or to tests of fact, and wants a free
hand.

Even more remarkable than Walpole's
authorship of such a story is Gray's critical admiration of it; and this once more can be ex-
plained only by remembering that Thomas
Gray, with all his shyness, with all his fastidious
scholarship, had completely surrendered to the
new Romantic Movement. His unbounded admiration for the first fragments of *Ossian*
(1760) made him an easy target, even for so
poor a shot as Walpole; for he welcomed at this
time everything in literature that savoured of
''wildness.'' He had seen the manuscript, and
advised his friend to print it; and when the book
appeared, he wrote to Walpole that it made people cry and afraid to go to bed o' nights. Thus

it produced the exact effect intended by all the works of this school—tears and terror—a combination of the school of sentiment with the school of mystery.

Tales that were meant to be thrilling now began to multiply; and we read to-day with a smile what our ancestors read with rising hair. Familiarity breeds contempt; and this is particularly true of ghosts. They must not appear too often or in too large numbers. But the thirst of the public for the uncanny had been aroused, and the main business of the second and third rate novelists was then, even as it is now, to satisfy a thirst. Clara Reeve's *Old English Baron* (1777), Ann Radcliffe's *Mysteries of Udolpho* (1794), and M. G. Lewis's *The Monk* (1795) are progressive examples of the fashion. Although not one of these books is worth reading for its own sake, they were a contribution to the stream of English fiction, and an evidence of the never-dying love of the English for romance. While great realistic novels, as faithful criticisms of life, may satisfy some of the people all of the time, and all of the people some of the time, they cannot satisfy all the people all the time.

There is another reason to-day why we may be grateful to these mystery-mongers. Just as *Pamela* was the mother of *Joseph Andrews,* so these hobgoblins gave birth to another immortal burlesque—*Northanger Abbey.* Jane Austen was only twenty-two when she wrote this story; and it was written in the flood-tide of the books it ridiculed, in the year 1798. In 1803 it was sold to a publisher in Bath, but perhaps the fashion in fiction was too strong for his cour-age, for he laid the manuscript away; years later, the family offered him the same amount that he had paid for the return of it; amazed and delighted, he lost no time in accepting. Then he was more amazed and less delighted by being informed of the author's name, already famous.

The sense of humour is the sure antidote for excessive sentiment and excessive improbabili-ties; as is shown by trying melodrama on a uni-versity audience. A huge Gothic galleon of romance may be successfully torpedoed by one joke. Many literary movements have found their limit—even in the most patient nations—by finally colliding with the public sense of humour; and it is certain that if the sense of humour were as well developed in the Russian people as the sense of tragedy, many of the contemporary abnormal novels would disappear in a burst of foam. Jane Austen—the most clearheaded woman who ever wrote fiction—found the atmosphere somewhat overheated; and the good-natured laughter of *Northanger Abbey* was like a draught of fresh air. It blew out the candles and brought daylight back to English fiction.

It is, of course, a good story well told, with real characters; but its purpose was to attack *The Mysteries of Udolpho* and the whole fashion of romance represented by that work. The anti-climax of the washing-bill is a youthful burlesque; but not content with this, in the sixth chapter we have *Sir Charles Grandison* rated above all the romances, together with a specific attack on Mrs. Radcliffe's tale. Apart from the historical interest of this satire, I find very in-

teresting the ironical treatment of the débutante
of 1798; and I think a citation will prove that
the twentieth century débutante has not radi-
cally changed.

Have you gone on with *Udolpho?*
Yes, I have been reading it ever since I woke; and
I am got to the black veil.
Are you, indeed? How delightful! Oh! I would
not tell you what is behind the black veil for the
world! Are not you wild to know?
Oh! yes, quite; what can it be? But do not tell
me. I would not be told on any account. I know
it must be a skeleton, I am sure it is Laurentina's
skeleton. Oh! I am delighted with the book! I
should like to spend my whole life in reading it, I
assure you; if it had not been to meet you, I would
not have come away from it for all the world.
Dear creature! how much I am obliged to you; and
when you have finished *Udolpho,* we will read the
Italian together; and I have made out a list of ten
or twelve more of the same kind for you.
Have you, indeed! How glad I am! What are
their names?
I will read you their names directly; here they are,
in my pocket-book. *Castle of Wolfenbach, Clermont,
Mysterious Warnings, Necromancers of the Black
Forest, Midnight Bell, Orphan of the Rhine,* and
Horrid Mysteries. Those will last us some time.

Yes; pretty well; but are they all horrid? are you sure they are all horrid?

Yes, quite sure; for a particular friend of mine,—a Miss Andrews,—a sweet girl, one of the sweetest creatures in the world, has read every one of them. I wish you knew Miss Andrews, you would be delighted with her. She is netting herself the sweetest cloak you can conceive. I think her as beautiful as an angel, and I am so vexed with the men for not admiring her!—I scold them all amazingly about it.

There is nothing meretricious about Jane Austen except the alliterative titles of two of her novels; she stopped that business after her first two books, and we read and reread *Pride and Prejudice* with such enthusiasm that we find no difficulty in forgiving the author for its christening. For this work is one of the world's very few impeccable masterpieces.

Miss Austen was an absolute realist, and each of her books is a profound and accurate criticism of life. Declining to write a historical romance she wrote to her foolish counsellor, "I could no more write a romance than an epic poem. I could not sit seriously down to write a serious romance under any other motive than to save my life; and if it were indispensable for me to keep it up and never relax into laughing at myself and other people, I am sure I should be hung before I had finished the first chapter.''

Although it would be false to say that her aim in writing stories was a didactic one, it is nevertheless true that, in common with her master Richardson, she meant to improve social manners, and her novels are in a sense books of etiquette. She was disgusted with the foolish and trivial and ill-written letters that passed between young girls in society; she was thoroughly indignant with fond fathers and mothers who made their little children protagonists of the family drama, as is so often the case to-day; she could not endure to have the children's conversation quoted, to have the good talk of adults lowered to the level of infants who happened to be in the room, nor to see a number of men and women surrounding a child, and talking baby-talk to its unconscious face. And while she probably loved Elizabeth Bennet more than any other of her characters, saying playfully of her, ''I must confess that I think her as delightful a creature as ever appeared in print; and how I shall be able to tolerate those who do not like *her* at least, I do not know," she perhaps meant Anne Elliott in *Persuasion* as her ideal of what a young girl should be.

The change that has taken place in a hundred years, not merely in our ideal girl but in the girl-ideal, can happily be illustrated by comparing the Anne Elliott of *Persuasion* with the Anne Elliott of *The Guest of Quesnay,* written by our deservedly popular American novelist, Booth Tarkington. Both girls spell their name the same way; each is meant to be attractive and representative; and the similarity of spelling together with the contrast in temperament made me feel certain that the comparison was intentional, until I was informed by Mr. Tarkington that it was wholly unconscious. The modern girl is healthy and capable; her face, neck, and hands are heavily tanned; on the inside of her hands there are callous mounds, caused by tennis, golf, and steering-wheels; much of the form divine is revealed by modern clothes; her language is an epitome of the latest argot; and Mr. Granville Barker says her walk, her gestures, and her manner are all an exact imitation of contemporary musical comedy. The attempt of most novelists is to make the heroine attractive; and I remember reading a review of Richard Harding Davis's *Soldiers of Fortune*, where in a discussion of how Hope Langham rose to a certain emergency, the reviewer exclaimed, "Hope did her stunt without a whimper." Now imagine Sophia Western— to illustrate from a very male novelist—doing her stunt without a whimper! Imagine Clarissa driving a motor! Why is it we never hear the word "Tomboy"—so common in my youth —applied to the modern girl? Simply because all girls nowadays are tomboys. The late Mr. Lounsbury said that Cooper's heroines were a combination of propriety and incapacity. I would not say that the modern heroine is improper—but simply that she would have seemed so to her sister of a century agone.

For the fact is, that just as there are styles in clothes so there are styles in character, in manners, yes, in the female body. In the twen-

tieth century thin girls are all the rage, so that
the reputation of Rubens as a painter has sunk
to such a depth that even the most ignorant
American tourists know that he is not to be
praised. This has not always been the case;
Charles Reade did not hesitate to give the leg
of Christie Johnstone a "noble swell"; he would
pare her down to-day. The modern heroine is
thin to angularity; when meant to be *very* attractive, her figure is called "boyish"; and
among the many trials of women, I should think
the necessity of changing their bodies to fit
fashionable requirements was not the least.
Bad enough to have such caprices in garments;
but to have your figure out of style! Still, it is
not so bad as being a dog; for if you are a dog
and are not in style, you simply are not born at
all. You cease to exist. What has become of
all the coach-dogs and Spitz dogs of my youth?
They went out of style and out of life simul-
taneously.

Now the eighteenth century fashionable girl
was most gentle, most proper, most retiring.
Her chief charm was delicacy; and if she had a

touch of tuberculosis, she became irresistible. This was the kind of young woman worshipped by our ancestors; to whom the modern Booth Tarkington girl would have been physically repulsive, as repulsive as an aggressively mannish woman is still. Does it seem incredible that a whole generation of males can differ from another generation in their admiration of women, and in their susceptibility? Such is nevertheless a fact. Fenimore Cooper, whose "females" are a mark for modern satire, was simply carrying the eighteenth century ideal to its limit. America has always been more conservative than England; perhaps for the same reason that a bourgeoise is much more careful in her "company manners" than a duchess. Cooper's heroines, like real eighteenth century ladies, faint with the greatest ease and with perfect technique; and as to their modesty, our novelist said of one of his creations, "on one occasion her little foot moved," although "she had been carefully taught too that even this beautiful portion of the female frame should be quiet and unobtrusive." Many readers, impatient at such drivel, think that Cooper must have been an ass. He was nothing of the kind; he was following the fashion. If he should revisit the glimpses of the moon, it would be worth while to guide him to Atlantic City or Coney Island.

Although the boldest of eighteenth century reformers would have been shocked by our modern girls, the ideal of physical incompetence and shy delicacy did not maintain its supremacy without a protest. And, as Professor Cross has shown, the first real rebellion broke out in that marvellous monitor of youth, *Sandford and Merton* (1783-1789), by Thomas Day. No sickly females for him! "She rises at candle light in winter, plunges into a cold bath, rides a dozen miles upon a trotting horse or walks as many even with the hazard of being splashed or soiling her clothes . . . " Jane Austen had so much common sense that she meant her Elizabeth to be a rebuke to the over-fastidious. "To walk three miles, or four miles, or five miles, or whatever it is, above her ankles in dirt, and alone, quite alone! what could she mean by it?

It seems to me to show an abominable sort of conceited independence, a most country-town indifference to decorum.''

Although Jane Austen's robust contemporary, Walter Scott, sometimes made his heroines act and talk in a way that seems to us insipid, his best girls are full of vigour, both of body and of mind. Mr. Saintsbury had the courage to name five nineteenth-century women whom he would have been glad to marry. They are Elizabeth Bennet, of *Pride and Prejudice;* Diana Vernon, of *Rob Roy;* Beatrix Esmond; Argemone Lavington, of *Yeast;* and Barbara Grant, of *David Balfour.* Most of these girls, while not reaching the cover standard of the contemporary American magazine, are active and capable; and among all of Scott's creations, it is notable that the modern critic selected Di Vernon, the all-around athlete.

The Romantic Revival of the eighteenth century reached a tremendous climax in Walter Scott. By virtue of his immense power and range, and unlimited creative activity, he remains the King of Romanticists. He belongs of course to the objective side of romanticism, as Byron belongs to the subjective; Scott is romantic in his material, Byron romantic in his mood. The great streams of Gothicism, Chivalry, and Mystery, as seen in architecture, ballads, and wild fiction, all united in the work of the Wizard. His achievement in prose romance is incomparably better than that of all his immediate predecessors put together, and had indeed no equal in English literature since the time of Malory.

Scott is the great impromptu in fiction, as Browning is in poetry; all of his work seems extempore. Naturally, therefore, he does not serve as a model of style. Stevenson, who had nothing but adoration for Scott's character, and his marvellous inventive powers, never forgave him for his carelessness in manner. "It is undeniable," said he, "that the love of the slapdash and the shoddy grew upon Scott with success." Of one of his sentences, Stevenson remarked, "A man who gave in such copy would be discharged from the staff of a daily paper. . . . How comes it, then, that he could so often fob us off with languid, inarticulate twaddle?''

Mark Twain, a careful and painstaking artist, had nothing but contempt for Scott until he happened to read *Quentin Durward*. He had been ridiculing the professors and the critics for their praise of Sir Walter, insisting that the so-called great man not only was insufferably dull, but that he did not even know how to write. Then he read *Quentin Durward,* which fascinated him so powerfully that he playfully insisted it had come from another hand. While it was impossible for Mark Twain to write any essay in criticism without grotesque exaggeration, there is some truth both in his condemnation of Scott and in the exception noted. If I were condemned to read all of Scott's novels again (a fearful punishment) I should look upon *Quentin Durward, Ivanhoe, The Bride of Lammermoor,* and *Kenilworth* as notable mitigations. Indeed, for sheer dramatic power, *The Bride of Lammermoor* is one of the greatest romances in the world. Many years ago, Sir William Fraser was engaged in a warm discus-

sion of Scott with Bulwer-Lytton. Finally, Sir
William proposed that each man write on a slip
of paper what he conceived to be Scott's masterpiece, at the same time expressing the utmost
confidence that they would write the same title.
They did; it was *The Bride of Lammermoor.*

Many of Scott's novels I find unreadable. I
cannot get through the underbrush. Over and
over again I have attacked *Woodstock,* always
in vain, and I shall never try any more. What
is there about such dreary romances, filled with
long descriptions and interminable meander-
ings, that conquers children? When I was a
child, I read Scott and Cooper with intense interest, never skipping a word. I rose before
dawn to read Cooper's *Two Admirals,* thinking
of it with anticipatory delight as I fell asleep;
I should exact favourable terms for reading it
now.

Scott, like all the great Romantics, was a
mighty man, and much of his production has immortal life. Somehow a writer may be a great
realist and yet not impress us with his vitality; may indeed seem anæmic. But the

great Romantics—Scott, Victor Hugo, Dumas,
Cooper, Sienkiewicz,—men who find this world
too cramped, and are forced to make their own
world, where they can have elbow-room—these
always give the impression of endless force.
The physical exception, Stevenson, had such
amazing mental vitality that if his bodily frame
had been powerful, he would probably never
have written a line; would perhaps have gone
to perdition by the shortest available route.
Readers who knew nothing of him always
imagined him healthily robust. The other Romantics had concealed within their mortal clay
some inextinguishable fire; on the coldest winter
day, Dumas would sit by an open window with
his coat off, writing novels, while the sweat
poured down his face. Victor Hugo, when he
ate a lobster, ate it all, insisting that the hard
shell aided his digestion, as he crumpled it in
his strong teeth. When he ate an orange, he
ate it as a boy eats an apple, skin and all. The
great Romantics are supermen.

And this vital flame blazes forever in their
masterpieces. Why is it that so many of our

modern romances, which sell for some years by the hundred thousand, disappear with a rapidity that must to their authors be disconcerting, while *The Three Musketeers, Ivanhoe, Notre Dame,* and *The Last of the Mohicans* are being read by thousands of people while I am writing this sentence? It is because, with all their carelessness of diction, with all their blemishes and incongruities, they are rattling good stories; stories that, told in the crudest manner about a campfire, would hold every auditor breathless; and because they contain characters so filled with the breath of life that a reader can no more forget them than he could forget his most intimate friend.

CHAPTER V

THE MID-VICTORIANS

The greatest decade in English fiction—hunting in couples —Dickens—his popularity in Russia—Thackeray the sentimentalist—George Eliot—which is her best novel?—Anthony Trollope and his twentieth century reincarnation—few great women novelists—the Brontë sisters—smouldering passion —invention and imagination—Wilkie Collins—Conan Doyle —superiority of Americans in the short story—Irving, Poe, Hawthorne, Harte, O. Henry—contemporary Russian masters of the short story—reticence and dignity in American art.

Perhaps the greatest decade in the history of the English Novel was the period between 1850 and 1860 inclusive. The list of titles is more impressive than any comment thereupon. *David Copperfield, Bleak House, Little Dorrit, A Tale of Two Cities, Great Expectations, Pendennis, Esmond, The Newcomes, The Virginians, Scenes of Clerical Life, Adam Bede, The Mill on the Floss, Alton Locke, Hypatia, Westward Ho, Peg Woffington, Christie Johnstone, It Is Never Too Late to Mend, The Cloister and the Hearth, The Warden, Barchester Towers, Doctor Thorne, The Woman in White, Villette, The Professor, Tom Brown's School Days, John Halifax, The Ordeal of Richard Feverel, The Scarlet Letter, House of the Seven Gables, Blithedale Romance, The Marble Faun, Uncle Tom's Cabin.* In order to find a parallel to such a rapid production of masterpieces in English literature, we should have to go back to the best days of the Elizabethan drama. The mid-Victorian publishers lived in the golden age: and their regular announcements—which make interesting reading in the advertising pages of old weeklies—must have aroused golden anticipations.

In one hundred years from *Clarissa, Tom Jones,* and *Roderick Random,* the novel had advanced to full maturity, with the complexity and technique that accompany the complete development of any form of art.

Great writers often come in pairs, and hunt the public in couples. Richardson and Fielding, Scott and Jane Austen, Dickens and Thackeray, Hardy and Meredith, Tennyson and

Browning, Goethe and Schiller, Turgenev and Tolstoi, Ibsen and Björnson, Hauptmann and Sudermann—to mention only some of the modern instances. A good thing this twinning seems to be for literature; genius echoes genius, and each rival spurs the other to his best.

Scott died in 1832; and within four years Englishmen were reading *Pickwick Papers,* the inspired writing of a new novelist, who had two great qualities not mainly characteristic of Sir Walter—humour and humanitarianism. Never was a man more kind to individuals than the great Scot; but his professional work resembles a long picture gallery, whereas the novels of Dickens make one glorified stump speech, abounding in sympathy for the outcasts, and shining with fun. No voice like this had ever been heard in English Literature; and for thirty years after his death, his silence was almost audible, till he returned to earth and dwelt among us as William De Morgan.

Of all British novelists, none has been more purely creative than Dickens; his tears flow from the great source, the sentimental novel of the eighteenth century, the only link between him and Sterne; but the pathos of Dickens is what the twentieth century finds least admirable in his work. He regarded his own childhood with considerable and justifiable self-pity; but his unfathomable tenderness is shown with especial force toward all children. The sufferings of little boys and girls made to him an irresistible appeal; and he felt that the death of a child was the most tragic event in nature, as Poe thought the death of a young girl the most poetically and romantically beautiful. Dickens insisted on the inherent dignity of childhood— a dignity constantly outraged both by the selfishness and by the condescension of adults.

Although Dickens had an enormous influence on the literature of the Continent, the only foreign novelist who resembled him both in genius and in temperament was Dostoevski. The title of one of the latter's stories, *The Insulted and Injured,* might almost be taken as the subject of the complete works of both writers. Both had suffered terribly in earliest youth; both knew the city slums; both knew the very worst of which humanity is capable; both loved humanity with a love that survived every experience; both were profoundly spiritual, intensely religious, and thoroughly optimistic. For the great artists who have known suffering and privation are more often optimists than those whose lives have been carefully sheltered. The game of life seems to be more enjoyed by those who play it than by those who look on.

Tolstoi and Dostoevski read Dickens with eagerness and profit. Dickens has been and is to-day more popular in Russia than any other English novelist; the common people feel their kinship to him in the touch of nature. In one of the Siberian provincial jails, where records are always kept of the prisoners' reading, the library minutes for 1914 are interesting. Of British authors in Russian translations, Dickens was called for 192 times; Scott, 98; Wells, 53; Wilde, 44; Kipling, 41; Shakespeare, 33.

In the history of British fiction, Dickens fills the biggest place, contributed the largest number of permanently interesting characters, owed less to other authors than any other novelist, and would be the one I should keep if all but one had to perish. No other writer has made so great a contribution to the greatest happiness of the greatest number; and while it is possible to contemplate the history of the novel minus any other author, we simply cannot get along without Dickens. The extraordinary succession of masterpieces that he produced with hardly any lapses for thirty years put the whole world hopelessly in his debt. He was the most creative and the least critical of all our writers of fiction; he attempted no formal essays; his *American Notes* ought not to have been written, and his *Child's History of England* would have blighted the reputation of a lesser man. It is absurd to call his characters mere caricatures: he turned the powerful searchlight of his mind into many dark places, and his persons stand out against the background in a conspicuous glare. But if these people are not true, why is it that all observers since 1840 are continually pointing out persons who "look like characters from Dickens"?

Although the middle of the nineteenth cen-

tury saw the Novel playing successfully the
rôle of life's interpreter, nearly every prominent writer felt bound to produce one historical
romance.   Dickens lacked everything but imagination in this field, and to me *A Tale of Two
Cities* is the poorest of all his stories, with the
one exception of *Little Dorrit.* As soon as he
had shaken himself free from it, he wrote one
of the best novels in English literature—*Great
Expectations;* even as Stevenson, flinging aside
St. Ives, produced the unfinished masterpiece,
Weir of Hermiston. George Eliot also failed;
when all is said, *Romola* is a work of construction rather than creation, more ponderous than
splendid.   And as a study of moral decay, it is
not so impressive as Mr. Howells's *Modern Instance.*   Charles Reade was so successful, however, that *The Cloister and the Hearth* is worth
all the rest of his works put together—I wonder
if he realised before he died how immensely
better it is?   And it seems now, as if *Westward
Ho* would outlast the more sensational and
formerly more popular *Hypatia.* For Charles
Kingsley was an Elizabethan by nature, and

was more at home with the seadogs of Devonshire than in a joint debate with Newman. It remained for Thackeray to write the best historical romance in our language, *Esmond*.

This book is almost entirely free from Thackeray's worst faults: his sentimentalism, his diffuseness, his personal intrusions on the stage. The story is told in the first person, which shut out the author: it was published as a whole in book form instead of being dragged out in monthly numbers; and it is a narrative so full of passion—real passions, love, jealousy, lust, revenge,—that there is no room for anything less vital. He wrote *Esmond* at white heat in a short time, and the manuscript shows few corrections. I like it best because it contains the best of Thackeray—and the best of Thackeray has not been surpassed in English fiction.

Thackeray's mind was more critical than that of Dickens: he was a natural-born critic, parodist, burlesquer, commentator. He walked the garden of this world and his novels—except *Esmond*—are gigantic commentaries on what he saw. Never was a writer less of a cynic and satirist than Thackeray; no doubt, like many people, he thought he was very severe; but as a matter of fact, he was a sentimentalist and a preacher, who loved humanity, saw its follies with the sharp sight of the humourist, and wished all the time that he could say something to make his readers profit by his personally conducted tours.

He was a chivalrous, magnanimous, tender-hearted, essentially noble character; no English novelist has ever better deserved the grand old name of gentleman. He confessed his sins against art like a man. "Perhaps of all the novel-spinners now extant, the present speaker is the most addicted to preaching. Does he not stop perpetually in his story and begin to preach to you?" He really missed the point of the objection to this practice. It is not that we are eager to hear what happened next and want no interruption: it is that these interruptions destroy the illusion, and are, from the artistic point of view, deplorably insincere. For this reason, I find *The Newcomes* an unreadable book. He wrote it frankly for cash, and said so.

Of the three great mid-Victorians, George Eliot was less rich in natural endowment than either Dickens or Thackeray, but wrote with more soberness of mind. She said she was neither pessimist nor optimist, but called herself a meliorist. Be this as it may, her books were all written in shadow, and have none of the abounding cheerfulness of Dickens, nor the lambent humour of Thackeray. Her humour, of which she had a plenty, was grave and ironical; no one has better depicted middle-aged women who combine vacuity of intellect with venomous selfishness. In fact I think no novelist has ever better depicted the unloveliness and corroding force of selfishness.

In true human pathos, her *Scenes of Clerical Life* were a revelation in English literature. What an enormous contrast between these depths of tragedy and the eighteenth century pools of sentiment! The restraint shown by the author emphasised the dignity of suffering. And one has only to compare young Maggie

Tulliver with Little Nell to see George Eliot at her best and Dickens at his worst. The constant attrition under which Maggie suffered is more painfully real to us than Nell's melodramatic and elaborate preparations for the tomb.

The Mill on the Floss leaves the tricks of realism and enters the field of reality. It is a noble, permanent example of the psychological novel, which had been started by Richardson. It would be difficult to find outside of Turgenev any love scenes in fiction which combine less carnality with more passion than the scenes between Stephen and Maggie. And it is not surprising that Turgenev admired this book. For once upon a time three men, Mr. George H. Lewes, Professor Boyesen of Columbia, and the Russian Turgenev were engaged in a warm discussion as to which one of George Eliot's novels was the best. Mr. Lewes declared for *Daniel Deronda,* the husband naturally thinking her latest was her finest; Professor Boyesen voted for *Middlemarch,* as being richest in content; but the great Russian, who valued correct analysis and profound sincerity above all other qualities in fiction, gave his opinion for *The Mill on the Floss*. I think Time is on his side.

George Eliot's last novel, *Daniel Deronda,* is over-weighted with opinion and propaganda, and is visibly sinking beneath the surface of literature. I wish I knew how many people had read it through in 1915! She wrote no more novels, and I do not think she could have written another. The best scenes in this book are the terrifying conversations between Grandcourt and Gwendolen, which I have always suspected were inspired by Browning's poem, *My Last Duchess*. The refinement of cruelty is so truthfully portrayed that one shudders as if present at a scene of torture.

Anthony Trollope's *Autobiography* is more interesting than his stories, and more improbable. There has never existed a less pretentious artist. He tells us exactly how his work was done, and we know nothing whatever about it. He said he would not be read in the twentieth century, but he is; even the enormous amount of his production—I saw an edition in

eighty-eight volumes—has not swamped his
reputation. Hawthorne's criticism of him accounts for his permanence; his novels are just
like life, some of them being so dull that we fly
to other books. No one would dare call Trollope a genius, and he would have ridiculed such
an appellation. It is rather singular that this
uninspired Englishman, in a grey business suit,
is so much more conspicuous in the history of
fiction than many gesticulating sensationalists
like Hall Caine; and it will be food for reflection if he should eventually outlast so brilliant
a dandy as Bulwer-Lytton.

Anthony Trollope has had a curious and altogether charming reincarnation in the twentieth
century in the person of Archibald Marshall,
whose novels may be confidently recommended
to admirers of *Barchester Towers*. Where does
Mr. Marshall get that skill—absent from English literature since Trollope's death—of rep-
resenting ordinary events and ordinary characters, not one of whom is wholly good or wholly
bad, in a way that makes the reader follow with
tense interest, unwilling to skip a word? The

trilogy of the Clinton family, and *Exton Manor,
The Greatest of These, The Old Order Chang-
eth* are good stories well told—I for one wish
they were twice as long.   These books have not
got the "punch," nor any "red blood," nor any
lubricity or vulgarity.   Strangest of all qualities, they are filled with charming, decent, well-
bred, kindly, human people, so that to read
these novels is like visiting in a good home.   Instead of being forced to associate with dull,
coarse, dirty loafers, whom one would not pick
for acquaintances in every day life, the reader
is brought into contact with extremely attractive men and women.   No one ought to quarrel
with Mr. Marshall for his principle of choice—
since readers and critics who prefer to spend
their time in the slums, in the antiseptically
safe way of realistic fiction, have constant and
abundant opportunity to do so.   I think that
it is more difficult to write any one of Mr. Marshall's novels than it is to produce the vast
majority of tales dealing with criminals and
abnormal villains.   And   our   contemporary
Trollope is really "true to life"; for the world

does actually contain some persons whom it is a pleasure to meet.

It is a rather curious fact that in the history of fiction in all languages, only two women have risen to the first rank—Jane Austen and George Eliot. This is the more odd because the art of the novel is to a certain extent imitative and critical, not nearly so purely creative as the art of musical composition, where no women of genius have ever appeared. Although not to be compared with the two names I have mentioned, the three Brontë sisters still have a place of their own in English literature. Anne now shines only by reflected light; few read *Agnes Grey,* and none would read it were she not the sister of Charlotte and Emily. The latter had perhaps the greatest natural endowment of the three; and *Wuthering Heights,* while more hysterical than historical in its treatment of human nature, has at any rate the strength of delirium. It was written by one who had passed, like old Dr. Donne, through the straits of fever—*per fretum febris.* It is short-sighted criticism that wonders at the mental range of passion of a girl

shut up in dreary loneliness; her capacity for
expression is what is remarkable, her passionate intensity exactly what one might expect
from such stifling repression. It is ridiculous
to believe that a woman's passions are passive
and not active; that she is unaware of them until some man appears on the scene; or that even
then her love is the love of reciprocation, that
cannot be roused independently of purposeful
masculine attention. Such ideas may make a
fancy virginal picture pleasing to some persons, but they are exactly contrary to the facts
of human nature. The recent publication of
Charlotte's love-letters ought to open the ears
of the deaf; but then, if they hear not Moses
and the prophets, neither will they be persuaded
though one rose from the dead.

Emily's narrow bodily existence fanned the
flames in her soul; and she could have counted
herself a queen of infinite space, had she not
had bad dreams.

Charlotte Brontë used in her novels her
Yorkshire and her Continental experiences; but
chiefly when she wrote, she looked into her

heart, as is indeed the way with most novelists of distinction. Most novels are really auto-biographies, and did we know as much about the external and spiritual life of all writers of fiction as we do of Tolstoi's, I think we should find often an equally faithful following of experience, though with less genius for recording it. Charlotte and her sister Emily wrote novels of revolt, expressing the hatred of that conventionality submitted to by so many women with such inner dissenting repugnance; for conventionality is such a tyranny that its bonds often become galling to women, every one of whom has the love of adventure in her heart; the desire for some thrilling excursion of the soul. Men of desperate valour seem to appeal to women more than those who are wise and prudent. No woman can endure a man who has too much caution. The little school-mistress in *Quality Street* loved the "dashing" officer—loved him and no other.

The fiery energy of Charlotte Brontë caused *Jane Eyre* to attract as much attention as a conflagration; it blazes still. She is a torch in literature rather than a fixed star. After she is extinguished the world will still be reading *Pride and Prejudice* and *Silas Marner*. To turn even now from *Jane Eyre* to these books is like passing from a vivid dream to reality.

Professor Brander Matthews has somewhere or other called attention to the distinction between invention and imagination, showing that while we may admire the cleverness of great inventive ingenuity, and while this gift may bestow upon its author immense temporary vogue, it does not, never has, and cannot place him with the immortal gods. A story ought to be the foundation of a novel; but a novel does not become immortal through a good plot. An excellent illustration of this is seen if one places side by side Wilkie Collins and George Eliot. As an inventor and manipulator of plot intricacies, we knew not the equal of Collins till Conan Doyle appeared. *The Woman in White, Armadale, The Moonstone*—marvellous, indeed, is the construction of these books. I sometimes think I have never seen a plot anywhere that rivalled in successful complexity the plot of *The Moon-*

stone. Suppose a good talker were to attempt to amuse and excite an audience by telling in his own fashion the outline of a famous novel— think of the contrast for such a purpose illustrated by *The Moonstone* and *The Mill on the Floss!* Yet there is not the slightest doubt that the latter is so much greater in literature that the two cannot even be named together. Collins was amazingly clever; each of his stories was an enigma, a delightful puzzle offered to the public. They brought him a vast number of readers and no fame—for Collins has no real fame; he hardly belongs to literature at all, except as a striking example of the school of mystery and horror. He felt himself that he was only an entertainer, and he made an effort to write a "purpose" novel, which he accomplished in *Man and Wife,* an attack upon college athletics and the marriage laws; but the only interest of this book is in its ingenuity. Critics would no more place Collins on a level with George Eliot, no, nor with Anthony Trollope, than they would rank on the platform a sleight-of-hand magician with Daniel Webster.

The wonderful mystery-criminal tales, dressed out in such gorgeous style by Poe, were developed prodigiously by Collins, who in our day has been almost obliterated from view by Conan Doyle. It would be difficult to exaggerate the popularity of this author. Sherlock Holmes is at this moment one of the best-known fictitious characters that has ever been created. And he is known in all languages, he has appeared on the stage in all countries. The Russians and the Japanese know their lean detective as well as the English. And yet, despite this universal vogue, despite our pleasure in these blood-curdling tales, despite our gratitude to the author for so many hours of delightful bewilderment, what would happen to the critic who should rank him among the great British novelists, or associate him in letters with another living Englishman, Thomas Hardy?

Such a state of things arouses reflection. It is clear that there must be something besides cleverness, even diabolical cleverness, to win anything like permanent fame.

In comparison between British and American

novelists—whether one takes the nineteenth or
the twentieth century—the patriotic American
would suffer actual pain, were it not that the
more patriotic a person is the more incapable
he is of seeing the truth.   Love is blind, love of
country stone-blind. But however harsh the
contrast in the domain of the novel, there is a
special province where America has actually ex-
celled England. This is seen in the production
of the Short Story, a species of art quite different, as has been pointed out, from the story that
is short. *Silas Marner* is a story that is short,
but not a Short Story; *The Gold Bug* is a Short
Story. Our first humourist, Washington Irving, occasionally attained unto perfection in this
difficult field. For in *Rip Van Winkle* and in
The Legend of Sleepy Hollow his narrative is
so good and his technique so perfect that the
world has agreed to regard these two as imper-
ishable classics. Irving's pathos seems thin
and flat to-day, and many of his meditative mus-
ings are staled by custom; but his humour,
quite English rather than American, is genuine,
and a marvellous preservative.

A world-genius followed Irving—Edgar Allan Poe. Poe's tales of mystery, in comparison with Cooper's tales of adventure, illustrate the analogy of the lyric and the epic. This analogy will not usually hold good; because the lyric represents one mood and is usually subjective, whereas Guy de Maupassant's short stories, for example, represent a variety of moods and are as near objectivity as it was possible for their gifted author to make them. But Poe was really a lyrical poet by nature; and the best of his short stories are almost perfect examples of prose lyrics. This becomes instantly apparent in reading *The Fall of the House of Usher* and (my own favourite) *Ligeia*. The sombre mood prevails, and rises to an agonising climax exactly as Tennyson's meditative rapture reaches a climax of passion in *Tears, Idle Tears*. The perfection of Poe's art, joined with the thrilling suspense of his plots, made him a world-figure, a fruitful influence in all countries. No foreign writer has reached the level of Poe's best work in the analysis of the passion he made his specialty—fear.

This level, however, is not the highest level. That was reached by Hawthorne, whose moral grasp of the realities of life gave to his short stories a firmer foundation and a broader and more lasting appeal. For while I have never outgrown Poe, I find that many others have, if they are telling the truth about it; it is impossible for any one to outgrow Hawthorne. The difference between Poe and Hawthorne is the difference between the uncanny and the spiritual; in human emotion, it is the difference between realism and reality. Poe makes our flesh creep with sensations; Hawthorne penetrates into the depths of our souls. Hawthorne used only the smallest fraction of his material; and to understand his method and his aim, it is necessary to read only *Ethan Brand*.

Bret Harte was another master of the short story, and a germinal writer as well. He found more gold in California than any of the miners, and he had a private mint of his own, by which he made it current coin, good wherever the soul of man is precious. His two best tales, *The Luck of Roaring Camp* and *The Outcasts of*

Poker Flat, are as vivid now as then; their drama and their pathos are real, approaching the line of melodrama and sentimentality without once stepping over.

In North Carolina they have just erected a statue to "O. Henry." He was a profoundly sincere artist, as is shown, not only in his finished work, but in his private correspondence. His worst defect was a fear and hatred of conventionality; he had such mortal terror of stock phrases, that as some one has said, he wrote no English at all—he wrote the dot, dash, telegraphic style. Yet leaving aside all his perversities and his whimsicalities, and the poorer part of his work where the desire to be original is more manifest than any valuable result of it, there remain a sufficient number of transcripts from life and interpretations of it to give him abiding fame. There is a humorous tenderness in *The Whirligig of Life,* and profound ethical passion in *A Blackjack Bargainer.* A highly intelligent though unfavourable criticism of Porter that came to me in a private letter—I wish it might be printed—condemns him for the

vagaries of his plots, which remind my corre-
spondent of the quite serious criticism he read
in a Philadelphia newspaper, which spoke of
"the interesting but hardly credible adventures
of Ulysses." Now hyperbole is a great American failing; and Porter was so out and out
American that this disease of art raised
blotches on his work. Yet his best emphasis is
placed where it belongs.

No writer of distinction has, I think, been
more closely identified with the short story in
English than O. Henry. Irving, Poe, Hawthorne, Bret Harte, Stevenson, Kipling attained
fame in other fields; but although Porter had
his mind fully made up to launch what he hoped
would be the great American novel, the veto of
death intervened, and the many volumes of his
"complete works" are made up of brevities.
The essential truthfulness of his art is what
gave his work immediate recognition, and accounts for his rise from journalism to literature. There is poignancy in his pathos; deso-
lation in his tragedy; and his extraordinary
humour is full of those sudden surprises that

give us delight.   Uncritical readers have never
been so deeply impressed with O. Henry as have
the professional, jaded critics, weary of the old
trick a thousand times repeated, who found in
his writings a freshness and originality amount-
ing to genius.

Among the thousands of short stories written
by lesser Americans than the five mentioned
above, two by Richard Harding Davis will certainly be read for many years to come—*Galla-
gher,* the wonderful boy who "beat the town,"
and *The Bar Sinister,* which seems already to
have won its way into the select canine classics
of the world.

Russia, a country that has taught the world
more about realistic novels than any other, and
which has supplied the world with the best illustrations of the art, has also been pre-eminent
for the last hundred years in the short story,
her later writers achieving their highest fame
in this field.   Pushkin, the founder of modern
Russian literature, is the originator, as seen in
his "other harmony" of prose; Gogol's *Over-
coat* had more influence on succeeding writers

than any other work; Turgenev's *Sportsman's Sketches* are beautiful specimens and exerted a powerful moral influence as well; Tolstoi's short stories are among the best ever written, inspired by the New Testament parables, which are themselves incomparable, the absolute despair of modern art; after Tolstoi, the most notable master of the short story in Russian is Chekhov, whose influence is just beginning to be felt in America; and if any one feels a doubt as to the excellence of the modern Russians, one should read Garshin's *Four Days,* Andreev's *Silence,* Gorki's *Twenty-six Men and a Girl,* and Artsybashev's *Nina.* Every Russian novelist of distinction has written admirable short stories except Dostoevski. As the American defect is humorous exaggeration, so the Russian defect is tragic exaggeration—it might be a wholesome corrective for each nation to study the best art of the other. Unfortunately, though quite naturally, the only American short stories that are really popular in Russia are the evil dreams of Edgar Allan Poe.

Although we have no young Americans who

can compare with Andreev, Sologub, Artsybashev, Gorki, Kuprin, there is one respect in
which American short stories and indeed all
American fiction in general show superiority
to the Russian; and I am fully aware that what
I regard as our chief merit is precisely the thing
for which we are most stridently condemned.
I mean our reserve in depicting the passion of
sex. We have been scourged for this not only
by foreign writers, but by many of our "advanced" journalists; it is incidentally well to
remember that not one of these American men
and women who ridicule the work of Mr.
Howells and Mr. James has ever written anything that approaches it in literary distinction.
We ought not to be ashamed of the American
reverence before the mystery of passion; we
ought to regard it with pride. We have
scarcely any outrageously indecent authors,
whose work, common enough in Europe, bears
about the same relation to true art that a boy's
morbid sketches on fences bear to Michael An-
gelo's frescoes. Indecency is not necessarily
sincerity. Instead of omitting the *motif* of

passion in art, instead of ignorance, timidity, or prudishness, our American reticence really indicates a better appreciation of its tremendous force. For as Henry James once pointed out, the silence of the American before the mysteries of passion shows more reverence than profuse and detailed exhibitions. It shows more reverence, more understanding, and more dignity.

Our American literature is sadly in need of improvement, but we shall not improve by imitating the only thing in Continental literature which takes no talent to copy. Changing the trumps will not help us nearly so much as more skill in playing the game.

CHAPTER VI

ROMANTIC REVIVAL 1894–1904

The romantic revival from 1894 to 1904—Zola and Stevenson—two predictions of approaching romance—the remarkable year 1894—Weyman, Doyle, Hope, Churchill, Stockton—Sienkiewicz—passing away of romantic extravagance—survivals of the school, such as McCutcheon and Farnol—the "life" novel of to-day—DeMorgan, Bennett, Wells, White, Rolland—the gain to the novel—the loss.

WHEN George Eliot died in 1880, it appeared as though English fiction would not soon burst the fetters of Realism. Dickens, Thackeray, George Eliot, Trollope, and Reade, despite an occasional holiday in the climate of romance, were all professional realists; Thomas Hardy was attracting a steadily widening circle of readers; in America, Howells and James were busily a-hunting specimens with the camera; Turgenev and Tolstoi were stimulating the British novel in French-translation-dilutions; and in France, this very year saw the publication of Zola's treatise on the Experimental Novel.

Romance seemed anachronistic. Zola, flushed with the new scientific spirit, wholly confident that he belonged to the future and the future to him, announced that Walter Scott was a novelist exclusively for boarding-school girls! that he would never again be read by serious and mature readers.

Zola was merely announcing what seemed to the majority of his listeners, irrefragably true. Two factors, however, were overlooked in his prophecy,—which may be called the negative and the positive element. Realism and romanticism seem bound to alternate; and the realists were so overconfident, so sure of themselves, that they plunged into excesses inevitably certain to lead to reform, or at any rate to something different. It is a great pity that Zola could not have lived to describe his own death; for the manner of his death would not only have interested him, it would have made a splendid chapter in any one of his experimental novels. It will be remembered that he died of suffocation in his sleep; he was found, in the morning, lying half out of bed, his face on the floor buried in his own vomit. The death of this great leader is an excellent illustration of the limits of his art.

The other factor—the positive factor—is not so easy to predict as the negative; but its possibility is always delightful to contemplate, for it makes the history of art to resemble a wonderful game of chance. When the citizens of the French Revolution thought they had established republican equality, Napoleon Bonaparte happened to appear on the scene; and when the giant Realism had got the spirit of English fiction safely locked into the dungeon, the young knightly figure of Stevenson arrived and released her.

Stevenson was thirty years old when George Eliot died. He looked about him on a dreary landscape. At its best, realism was made up of afternoon teas; at its worst, it was garbage. He wanted something that should at once be more stimulating and more agreeable. Not being able to discover it anywhere, he was forced to produce it himself. "For Zola," said he in a letter, "I have no toleration, though the curious, eminently bourgeois, and eminently French creature has power of a kind. But I would he were deleted. I would not give a chapter of old Dumas . . . for the whole boiling of the Zolas."

Stevenson said the following titles "should be": *The Filibuster's Cache: Jerry Abershaw: Blood Money: a Tale,* instead of "what is," *Aunt Anne's Tea Cosy, Mrs. Brierly's Niece, Society: a Novel.* It was about the year 1884 that he wrote this.

However, in 1881 he was sure of his mission. Although *Treasure Island* was not published until 1883, we find that he had begun work upon it so early as the 25th August, 1881, for on that day he wrote to Henley:

I am now on another lay for the moment . . . see here, *The Sea-Cook, or Treasure Island; a Story for Boys.* If this don't fetch the kids, why, they have gone rotten since my day. Will you be surprised to learn that it is about Buccaneers, that it begins in the *Admiral Benbow* public-house on Devon coast, that it's all about a map, and a treasure, and a mutiny, and a derelict ship, and a current, . . . and a doctor, and another doctor, and a sea-cook with one leg, and

a sea-song with the chorus "Yo-ho-ho and a bottle
of rum" (at the third Ho you heave at the capstan
bars), which is a real buccaneer's song, only known
to the crew of the late Captain Flint. . . . That's the
kind of man I am, blast your eyes. . . . And now
look here—this is next day—and three chapters are
written. . . . It's quite silly and horrid fun, and
what I want is the *best* book about the Buccaneers
that can be had . . . a chapter a day I mean to do;
they are short; and perhaps in a month *The Sea-
Cook* may to Routledge go, yo-ho-ho and a bottle
of rum! . . . No women in the story, Lloyd's orders;
and who so blithe to obey? It's awful fun, boys' stories; you just indulge the pleasure of your heart, that's
all; no trouble, no strain. . . . O sweet, O generous,
O human toils! You would like my blind beggar in
Chapter III, I believe; no writing, just drive along
as the words come and the pen will scratch!

Seldom is a preacher able to practise so well.
An ardent advocate of the gospel of romance,
Stevenson, in less than a dozen years, produced
*Treasure Island, Prince Otto, Kidnapped, The
Black Arrow, The Master of Ballantrae, Catri-
ona (David Balfour), The Ebb Tide.*

These books worked a revolution in English
fiction. One man, appearing at just the moment when readers were either weary or dis-

gusted with the reigning Sovereign, Realism,
toppled him over with the sheer audacity of
genius.   Many who read these lines can remember the mad eagerness with which we greeted
those new romances.   What a relief to turn
from the close, foul mugginess of naturalism to
the invigorating air of the ocean!   For Stevenson's immense service to letters was really
nothing more nor less than opening the windows
of heaven, and sweeping the chambers of art
with air and sunshine.   Before he died, he had
converted the English speaking world, and he
knew it.

It seems to me pedantic to prefer Scott to
Stevenson.   The latter beat the former at his
own game.   Stevenson's romances are more
thrillingly adventurous than Scott's; his characters are equally interesting; his style is im-
measurably superior.   When I first read *The
Beach of Falesà,* I had to stop and compose
myself, so loud was the beating of my heart.
His men and women will be my intimates for
the rest of my life.   And the great goddess of
Romance, hitherto rigged out in any old clothes,

was adorned by Stevenson with graceful, exquisite, and shining garments. It is safe to say that with the one exception of *Henry Esmond,* there has never been in the literature of prose romance so happy a blending of wildly exciting incident with such technically rhetorical perfection.

Of all modern authors, Stevenson is the best for youth. Our boys and girls follow the arch-magician from wonder to wonder, and they learn the delight of reading, and they absorb the beauty of style, as one learns good manners by associating with well-bred exemplars. For Henry James, describing a lady serving tea on an English lawn, is not more careful of his language than Stevenson, describing one-legged Silver in the act of murder. Stevenson was purely literary; he was not a great dramatist nor a great poet, though he wrote verses and plays; but it is abundantly clear that he was a great novelist, essayist, and maker of epistles. In these three departments he stands in the first rank.

Two years before his death the signs of the

coming revival of romance were unmistakable, and it is interesting to remember that two English critics went on record at almost the same moment. Mr. Saintsbury and Mr. Gosse each independently predicted the coming flood, warning all novelists to get into the ark of safety. In an essay called *The Present State of the English Novel* (1892), part of which had been printed in 1888, Professor Saintsbury hazarded the following definite but somewhat cautious prophecy:

In discussing the state of the English novel at a time which seems likely to be a rather exceptionally interesting one in the history of a great department of literature in England, it will probably be as well to make the treatment as little of a personal one as possible . . . the question . . . is one of setting in order, as well as may be, the chief characteristics of the English novels of the day, and of indicating, with as little rashness as possible, which of them are on the mounting hand and which are on the sinking. And for my part, and in the first place, I do not see any reason to think the reappearance of the romance of adventure at all likely to be a mere passing phenomenon. For the other kind has gone hopelessly sterile in all countries, and is very unlikely to be good for anything unless it is raised anew from seed, and

allowed a pretty long course of time. . . . All things
are possible in a time when a novelist of real talent
like M. Zola dismisses Sir Walter Scott as a "boarding-school novelist," and when a critic of real intelligence like my friend, Mr. Brander Matthews, takes
Mr. Howells for an excellent critic. The safer plan
is to stand still and see the wonderful works of the
Lord.

In an essay called *The Limits of Realism in
Fiction* (1893), Mr. Edmund Gosse remarked:

In the meantime, wherever I look I see the novel
ripe for another reaction. The old leaders will not
change. It is not to be expected that they will write
otherwise than in the mode which has grown mature
with them. But in France, among the younger men,
every one is escaping from the realistic formula. The
two young athletes for whom M. Zola predicted ten
years ago an "experimental" career more profoundly
scientific than his own, are realists no longer. M.
Guy de Maupassant has become a psychologist, and
M. Huysmans a mystic. M. Bourget, who set all the
ladies dancing after his ingenious, musky books, never
has been a realist; nor has Pierre Loti, in whom, with
a fascinating freshness, the old exiled romanticism
comes back with a laugh and a song. All points to a
reaction in France; and in Russia, too, if what we
hear is true, the next step will be toward the mystical
and the introspective. In America it would be rash

for a foreigner to say what signs of change are evident. The time has hardly come when we look to America for the symptoms of literary initiative. But it is my conviction that the limits of realism have been reached; that no great writer who has not already adopted the experimental system will do so; and that we ought now to be on the outlook to welcome (and, of course, to persecute) a school of novelists with a totally new aim, part of whose formula must unquestionably be a concession to the human instinct for mystery and beauty.

This scripture was fulfilled in our ears.

The year of Stevenson's death, 1894, was a notable year in the history of English fiction, both for the number and varied excellence of the novels it produced; and because it was the beginning of a tidal wave of romanticism. Old faiths always flash brightest just before their extinction, thinks Thomas Hardy; and in the year 1894, were published *Trilby, Marcella, Life's Little Ironies, Esther Waters, Lord Ormont and His Aminta, Pembroke,* which have nothing to do with any romantic reaction; but there also appeared *The Ebb Tide, The Jungle Book, Perlycross, The Tragedy of Pudd'nhead Wilson, Under the Red Robe, My Lady Rotha,* and a story of prodigious influence, *The Prisoner of Zenda.*

The demand for some of these books was so sharp and the rapidity of their circulation so remarkable, that the sales became a matter of interest to critics who were watching the public taste. It was about this time that the New York *Bookman* began to publish its monthly list of "best sellers," which not merely recorded the lines of popularity, but gave a stimulus to their extension.

Romanticism suddenly became so fashionable that many young men and women wrote their first attempts in fiction in this manner; and some novelists of established reputation, unwilling to be left adrift, trimmed their sails to the fresh breeze. The old masters, Hardy, Meredith, Howells, James, refused to surrender; but Hardy speedily stopped writing novels; so did Meredith; and in America there was so strong a reaction against Howells and James that for some years their readers greatly diminished in numbers, and their production in excellence. Mr. Howells, though he kept right on, wrote nothing of high value from 1892 to 1902; Mr. James produced little from 1890 to 1896—and in 1898, perhaps unconsciously under the influence of romance, he wrote one of the best ghost stories in the world, *The Turn of the Screw,* which is the wildest romanticism in a realistic setting. Mr. Howells protested in vain against this sudden domination of romance, calling the whole thing "romantic rot"; but while defiantly sceptical, he was nevertheless temporarily engulfed.

The strength of the Romantic Revival is shown most clearly in the fact that it drew men whose natural tastes, inclinations, and temperaments were realistic, and forced them to produce romances. Stanley Weyman, whose modest preface to the new edition of his works is confessionally charming, admits that he has tried merely to give entertainment to the public; and that if he has brightened lonely hours, he is satisfied. Now Mr. Weyman, by nature, is a realist, and he began his career with a novel that might have been written by Anthony Trollope. It is called *The New Rector,* and it is an excellent bit of pure realism. It made not the slightest impression; suddenly shifting, he produced in rapid succession, *The House of the Wolf*, *A Gentleman of France*, *Under the Red Robe*, and found himself one of the most famous men in the world. For about fifteen years he kept up a copious contribution, and when the romantic wave subsided, he retired.

My own experience on a certain Sunday evening in 1894 illustrates in microcosmic manner the world's change of heart from realism to romanticism. I had just finished reading *Marcella*, and I felt as if my mouth were full of ashes. Then I picked up *Under the Red Robe*, and I read it from first page to last not only without rising from my chair, but without a wiggle in it. Such a glorious relief from tiresome party politics and pharisaical reformers in London, to

"Marked Cards!"

the lie hotly given and returned, the tables and chairs overset, the rush for the dark street, the clash of swords, the parry and thrust—we're off!

The physician, Conan Doyle, with his finger on the public pulse, had already got started in the late eighties with *Micah Clarke* and *The White Company;* but these books were not nearly so much read in the eighties as in the nineties, when they were more in the fashion. Anthony Hope, who had been graduated from Balliol with scholarly honours of the first class, and whose real tastes and talents in literature are seen in the *Dolly Dialogues* and *Quisanté,* produced the romantic extravaganza, *The Prisoner of Zenda,* with his tongue in his cheek. This should have been turned into a comic opera, but so hot was the public for romantic excitement, that together with *Under the Red Robe,* it had an enormous run on the boards as sheer melodrama. I am glad that Mr. Hawkins wrote *The Prisoner of Zenda,* because it gave to so many people a pleasurable and innocent excitement; but I do not believe he would have written it either fifteen years before or fifteen years after. . . . It was a great mistake to kill the gentleman in *Rupert of Hentzau;* books

that are written for entertainment should not
suddenly become black.

The romantic germ crossed the ocean, and
America was infected. Historical romances
became amazingly popular; so long as they were
"costume novels," whose characters talked a
jargon of obsolete oaths, and had a sentimental
love story, with a historical royal personage
as *deus ex machina,* it mattered not if their historical foundation betrayed ignorance, nor if
their style were crude. Scores of such books
might be mentioned, which sold like wildfire
until the next sensation came along; but a
peculiarly excellent example of the whole class
appeared in *When Knighthood Was in Flower,*
by the late Charles Major. This work was
painfully lacking in distinction, yet over five
hundred thousand copies were sold. If Stevenson spoke contemptuously of his own poorest
bit of tushery, *The Black Arrow,* what would he
have said to this? It is fortunate that a
teacher cannot always be judged by the work of
his disciples.

Mr. Winston Churchill, now one of the most popular realistic novelists in America, who seems more interested in political, religious and social reform than in the art of the novel, and whose books sell by the hundred thousand, happened to begin his career in the flood-tide of the romantic revival; and being an infallible interpreter of public taste, naturally wrote an exciting historical romance, *Richard Carvel,* with a frontispiece of a duel in appropriate costume; this story, reminiscent in places of *The Virginians,* enjoyed a tremendous vogue. Now if one wishes to know how the temper of the reading public has changed from 1899 to 1915, one has merely to compare *Richard Carvel* with *The Inside of the Cup* or *A Far Country.*

The late Paul Leicester Ford, realist by instinct and training, whose *Honorable Peter Stirling* has not yet been forgotten (although the hero has been identified both with Grover Cleveland and David B. Hill), wrote a stirring historical romance, *Janice Meredith,* which conquered the public immediately, and like so many of its kind was speedily transferred to the stage and thence to oblivion.

Miss Mary Johnston's *To Have and to Hold,* coming at the end of the century, when the romantic movement reached its climax, had, but did not hold, a tremendous popularity. Being absolutely up to date, it rather quickly passed out of style. Booth Tarkington, a writer of great skill and talent, who had made a contemporary study of manners in *The Gentleman from Indiana,* contributed a charming *jeu d'esprit* to the romantic school in *Monsieur Beaucaire;* compared with Dumas's *Three Guardsmen,* this is a humming-bird to an eagle; yet its brightness has not faded with the passing summer of romance. This comparison, by the way, reminds me that just at the height of this fashion a new version of Dumas's immortal story was put on the American stage by Mr. Sothern, and flourished mightily.

Perhaps the centripetal force of the romantic movement is shown most clearly in America by the sudden catching up of our late beloved Frank Stockton. Humour acts on romance like prussic acid; and Frank Stockton was a professional humourist, whose most characteristic work—may it never die!—is *The Casting Away of Mrs. Lecks and Mrs. Aleshine*. Mr. Stockton had puzzled the world by his strange tale of *The Lady or the Tiger;* but he puzzled the critics much more when he wrote *The Adventures of Captain Horn,* a slam-bang yarn of blood and gold. Many of the critics thought he meant it as a burlesque. Mr. Howells, alarmed by this apparent defection of a notable novelist, insisted that the whole thing was a joke. But it was quite the contrary; it was a case of a trained literary expert following the market, seeming to say, "If you really want tales of adventure, why not have good ones?" And *Captain Horn,* which I have read four times, is one of the most ingenious and most thrilling of its kind. It had an enormous success, and unfortunately led its author into the composition of a sequel, which resembled most sequels. This *Captain Horn* is not only unlike Mr. Stockton's previous work, it represents a mental attitude flatly contrary.

The Romantic Revival lasted about fifteen years after Stevenson's death; and then, like most revivals, men returned to life, as after the rocket, we see the stars. There are certain American novelists, who, having started under the influence of *The Prisoner of Zenda,* do not quite see that this particular cock won't fight any more; such is the genial author of *Beverly of Graustark;* one of his novels had the following *aperitif* in the publisher's statement: "This book goes with a rush, and ends with a smash," —thus resembling neither life nor art. He is far better in sheer humorous extravaganza, like *Brewster's Millions.* A glaring English anachronism appears in the work of Jeffery Farnol.

More than thirty years have elapsed since the appearance of *Treasure Island;* yet, apart from the work of its author, I can think of not one historical romance among the hundreds that pullulated that seems likely to survive, except the splendid leviathans of Sienkiewicz. While Stevenson was writing his stories, the same mysterious spirit of romance hovered over

Poland, and in the eighties Henryk Sienkiewicz produced his great trilogy *With Fire and Sword, The Deluge,* and *Pan Michael.* These, translated by an admirable literary artist, the late Mr. Curtin, appeared in America in the early nineties, just at the psychological moment. Then in the year 1896 there was published the romance of Rome, *Quo Vadis,* the American translation coming from the press in Boston three months before the original in Warsaw. That particular year was a first-rate year for this kind of thing, and the world of historical romances had a bumper crop. This *Quo Vadis,* though decidedly inferior to the Polish trilogy, drew such wide and violent acclaim that it might just as well have been unanimous; and *The Last Days of Pompeii* has never seemed the same since. After this, Sienwiekicz's romances regularly appeared in English before Polish, in response to the keen demand. But is it a sign of the times? In 1900, at the climax of the romantic revival, *The Knights of the Cross* had a big sale, and it is indeed a noble work; but in 1906, when the movement was waning, *On the*

Field of Glory attracted little attention, and his subsequent works almost none at all; how many readers know of *Whirlpools* (1910) and *In Desert and Wilderness* (1912)? Yet these are assuredly worth reading.

Apart from the works of Stevenson and Sienkiewicz the romantic flood left no definite thing of value when it receded; but just as you can tell where a vanished stream has been by the bright freshness of the grass, so the influence of the romantic revival, in spite of its extremes of fashion, was healthful and refreshing. The novel went from realism to naturalism to experimentalism, and that way madness lies; then came a change in the weather, and the sultriness departed.

The old realism has not returned; but since the year 1906 a fine new spirit has entered into contemporary fiction, the spirit of Reality. The last ten years have been marked by a considerable number of long biographical novels, which I call for want of a better name, the "life" novel. Without the trappings and conventions of "realism," we find in this life school work that is thoroughly sincere. The basal interest in human nature is so great that even its weaknesses and trivialities have been always thought worthy of the serious attention of artists of dignity; and when faithfully reported, with sympathy, as by Thackeray, or with scorn, as by Flaubert,—immediately arouse in intelligent readers that delight of recognition which must ever be the target of the painter of portraits, whatever his implements may be. As Mr. Howells says, "Ah, poor Real Life, which I love, can I make others see the delight I find in thy foolish and insipid face?" He can; he has.

The new life school assume that every detail in their huge books will be interesting, so long as it can be verified by the experience of the reader. This is the secret of the wonderful charm of William De Morgan, who perhaps more than any other novelist, is responsible for the vogue of the lengthy biographical fictions of to-day. He had lived over sixty years without writing a page of creative work; he had scarcely read any novels except those of Dickens; was in

no sense of the word a literary man. If he had
not had an attack of influenza, he might not
have thought of writing; it was in the idleness
of convalescence that he began, and was domes-
tically persuaded to finish *Joseph Vance*. Even
then he came near cancelling the first chapter;
it seemed too much like Dickens. His novel
contained 280,000 words, and as Mr. De Morgan
writes an enormous hand, the bulk of his manuscript was appalling. He sent it to a publisher,
and immediately received it back, by freight, I
suppose. Thinking it might possibly be ex-
amined if in smaller proportions, he had it
"typed." One morning, as the chief entered
the room, he found the girl who was typing
Joseph Vance shaken with sobs; the story was
too much for her feelings. This made sufficient
data for Mr. William Heinemann, the most en-
terprising publisher in London; in the summer
of 1906 appeared *Joseph Vance,* which pur-
ported to be "an ill-written autobiography,"
and it took England and America by storm. It
narrates in the first person the biography of
Joseph Vance from babyhood to old age; its

descriptions are a mirror, its conversations an echo, of reality.

One of the most popular of British novelists at this moment is Arnold Bennett. The manner in which he won popularity is even more flattering to the public than to him. He had taken a rather cavalier air as a journalist, and could "see no harm" in writing stuff that he knew was trash, so long as one earned a living by it. He had the serious soul of the artist, and the mocking ironical spirit of the self-conscious literary trickster; some books, he frankly confessed, he wrote as pot-boilers, while in others he enjoyed the luxury of writing to please himself, that is, to please his conscience. Well, what happened? He had published *Anna of the Five Towns, The Grand Babylon Hotel, The Gates of Wrath, Leonora, A Great Man, Sacred and Profane Love, Whom God Hath Joined*,— all superficially clever works of no value, written to make money. But they did not make money. They did not make anything. No one in America apparently had ever heard of him until he published (just to please himself) the

sincere and tragic history of the lives of two
sisters, *The Old Wives' Tale* (1908). The sincerity and fidelity of its art were instantly recognised; and Mr. Bennett found himself a
famous man, with an immense public eager to
read anything from his pen. What happened?
This solid work not only gave him reputation
and money, it supported all his previous literary frivolities. What does it mean in his bibliography when we see after all those light ham-
mock-and-steamer books that I have mentioned,
the legend "New Edition," with a date invariably subsequent to 1908? What does it mean
when we find that some of them were not published at all in America until after 1908?

Not only was his most serious essay in art
the book that brought the harvest he had in vain
tried to reap, his subsequent works in lighter
vein were done with far greater skill. There is
simply no comparison in charm and cleverness
between *The Grand Babylon Hotel* (1902: new
edition, 1914: first printed in America, 1913),
and *The Card* (1911), published the same year
in America under the title *Denry the Audacious*.

Under any title it is one of the most delightful flashes of humour in our time; but what a detestable habit English writers have of changing the name of a book when it appears in the United States!

Like most successful English novelists of the twentieth century, Mr. Bennett is a successful playwright. His dramaturgic adventures must have interfered with the completion of the trilogy begun in 1910 with *Clayhanger,* and continued in 1911 with *Hilda Lessways,* as may be seen by remembering that *Milestones* appeared in 1912. Thousands of serious readers awaited with considerable eagerness the third book in this chronicle of commonplace and selfish lives, made to appear even more commonplace than any individual life really is. (This effect is attained simply by forgetting the spiritual values present in every person in the world.) The above-said serious readers waited until 1915, and I fear they are not certain that *These Twain* was worth the wait. It is marked by genuine artistic sincerity, its best quality; but perhaps success and vivid popularity have dulled the edge of Mr. Bennett's pen, as they certainly have for the moment clipped his wings. This latest history of people who eat and drink and sleep lacks the splendid zeal burning all through *The Old Wives' Tale*. It is a verification of Henry James's comment that in the work of Arnold Bennett we admire the patient and steady industry of the man, laying brick on brick, but it is impossible to guess for what object the structure is raised.

Has Mr. Bennett in this latest work really done his absolute best? His best is good, very good indeed; but he is not a bit too good for his public.

Mr. Wells, who is one of those infrequently born persons—a professional reformer and a professional humourist—has made one important contribution to the life novel, in *Tono-Bungay*, (1909), which may eventually rank as his most important work.

In America, one of the best examples of this school is seen in *A Certain Rich Man,* by William Allen White, of Kansas. The style of this story is somewhat careless; but it is a thoroughly sound book, pregnant with reality; one of the finest American novels of the twentieth century. It has little grace, and no lightness of touch; but it is a faithful picture of the life of an American, and is redeemed from clumsiness by the strength of sincerity.

Just as Naturalism was supplanted by Romanticism, so the absurd excesses of Romanticism were suicidal. It seems astonishing to remember that in 1894-1899 the typical novels were *The Prisoner of Zenda, When Knighthood Was in Flower,* and *Richard Carvel,* and that from 1906-1909 the public were devouring *Joseph Vance, The Old Wives' Tale, Tono-Bungay,* and *A Certain Rich Man.*

The new movement bore fruit, not to say a whole orchard, in one novel in France, *Jean Christophe,* by Romain Rolland. This is the detailed biography of one man, beginning with his birth-cry, and ending with the death-rattle. It was published in ten volumes, and has deservedly attracted more serious attention than any other French novel of this century. It has been translated into most European languages, and might well have been called *The Life and Times of Jean Christophe;* for it is a wonderful picture of the intellectual life in Europe before the Great War, and ought to be of permanent value. Its author has the French clearness of vision, with a New England conscience.

The one great defect in the life novel, seen of course most clearly in the immense number of feeble imitations of the books I have mentioned, is the temptation to formlessness. Many of them have no plot, and no sense of construction; they begin with birth, and might go on indefinitely; the author adding incidents until he has had enough, and then deciding to quit. He is either too lazy or too incompetent to provide an artistic structure. It is all well enough to write a biographical novel, but it ought to be a novel, not a biography nor a diary. The great horde of novel-writers follow the market so sharply that I am already becoming somewhat weary of stories, where, if you open the first chapter, you are in the nursery; the middle chapter, you are just leaving college; the last chapter, you hear bells—sometimes wedding, sometimes funeral. This kind of thing is getting to be altogether too common; I could name many, but I remember three rather popular novels, which appeared almost at the same moment in 1915, that illustrate, along with some excellent qualities, the chief defects and the wearisome repetition of this rather shiftless method.

CHAPTER VII

MEREDITH AND HARDY

George Meredith—his long career—his German education —false starts—spirit and body—his hatred of asceticism— his original force—his bad style—born in the wrong age —naturally adapted to poetic drama—his combination of paganism and optimism—his belief in the individual—the vagueness of his teaching—his hatred of discipline—his chivalry—*Rhoda Fleming*—normality of Meredith's characters—Clara Middleton—Meredith's impatient dislike of Tennyson—his criticism of himself in *Beauchamp's Career* —a fantastic genius—fluctuations of his reputation—his superb tribute to America—a footnote on Thomas Hardy.

A GIGANTIC and unique figure in modern fiction demands separate and serious attention. George Meredith died on the eighteenth of May, 1909, and "the air seems bright with his past presence yet." Although in his ideas and mental attitudes he was emphatically a man of the twentieth century, it is interesting and pleasant to remember that he published fiction before the earliest work of George Eliot appeared. None of his books ever had a large sale; but during the last twenty-five years of his life his name commanded immense respect, his home was a Mecca for literary men, and his death seemed like the falling of a pillar of literature. No modern writer has come before the public with higher "recommendations"; the much-abused word "master" is here fitly applied; and the verse tribute of Thomas Hardy and the prose poem of J. M. Barrie were beautiful flowers on his grave.

His birthday was the day of Darwin and Lincoln; his birth-year the year of Tolstoi and Ibsen; and even if his work cannot rank in importance with the work of these four, his personality shines with real splendour.

Although Meredith was born in Hampshire, England, and spent most of his life in the southern part of the island, his education and his temperament were decidedly un-English. He went neither to Oxford nor to Cambridge, but to Germany; did he unconsciously acquire there his cumbersome, involved and unmanageable style? For the only English author with whom his prose style has anything in common is

Thomas Carlyle, who was also inspired by Germany; and we know that Meredith had a towering admiration for Carlyle. Of course he did not really write like him; he wrote like no one. But the manner of his thinking, however unpalatable this may be just now, was German. He was more interested in the metaphysics of passion than in passion; and his novels are fully as much the product of speculative thought as of accurate observation. He spun all his books out of himself, as a spider spins his delicate and intricate web; this too is quite German; it is exactly the way Kant built the fabric of the *Kritik of Pure Reason.*

Whatever may be Meredith's place in the history of the novel, none can deny to him the title of original and powerful thinker.

Meredith's first essays at the profession of law and the business of marriage were alike unhappy and unsuccessful; he was by nature an absolutely free spirit. . . . His soul's dark cottage let in new light as he approached the grave; no one who saw him in his later years went away unimpressed. His noble and beautiful head, adorned with hair and beard of snow, made a presence of inexpressible dignity.

His chief recreation, apart from the foolish one of throwing and catching again a heavy hammer, which probably weakened his spine, was reading French literature. It is rather strange that he learned nothing from French style—the clear, precise, short sentences in that language ought to have affected him, and did not. But his attitude toward the French was wonderfully sympathetic; wonderfully so, because until the days of the *Entente* most Englishmen have signally failed to understand the French point of view. Look at the narrowness of Tennyson! But there was nothing insular about Meredith.

Like so many novelists, Meredith began his career as a poet, his first volume of poems appearing in 1851. He would rather have spent his life writing poetry than prose; but he had no money. Fiction was his kitchen wench, he always used to say; poetry was his Muse. His poems have received hysterical and rhapsodical praise, but he is not really among the English poets, and even if he were, it is none of our business here.

As Browning has observed, the bird wings and sings at the same time; spirit and body help each other; and just as a life of sensuality will surely deaden the spirit, so a life of asceticism in many cases has an effect somewhat similar. Meredith's genius was profoundly spiritual, but he believed the spirit expressed itself through the body. In a letter written in 1888, he said, "I have written always with the perception that there is no life but of the spirit; that the concrete is really the shadowy; yet that the way to spiritual life lies in the complete unfolding of the creature, not in the nipping of his passions. An outrage to Nature helps to extinguish his light. To the flourishing of the spirit, then, through the healthy exercise of the senses."

The intense and acrimonious difference of opinion about the value of Meredith's novels is an indication of the force of his personality, and of his unconventionality of expression. Browning, Wagner, Ibsen, aroused a tempest which has left a clear sky of fame; clouds and darkness are still around Walt Whitman. Meredith and Whitman are authors that it is best to treat pragmatically, if we wish their work to bear fruit in our souls; if you think they are respectively the greatest novelist and the greatest poet of modern times, why, then they are, to you.

To me George Meredith is neither God nor Devil. He is not my Teacher, as Browning is; not my Artist, as Hardy is; not my Refuge, as Stevenson is. But he was a genial giant, and I have for his manhood and his genius profound reverence. I know of no better illustration of the phrase Arnold applied to Emerson. George Meredith was not a great novelist; he was a great man who wrote novels. He was one of the greatest men of our time.

No criticism of him has pleased me more than that by the late Henry James. "The lyrical element is not great, is in fact not present at all in Balzac, in Scott . . . nor in Thackeray, nor in Dickens—which is precisely why they are so essentially novelists, so almost exclusively lovers of the image of life. . . . It is considerable in that bright particular genius of our own day, George Meredith, who so strikes us as hitching winged horses to the chariot of his prose—steeds who prance and dance and caracole, who strain the traces, attempt to quit the ground, and yearn for the upper air.''

Meredith wrote with the utmost difficulty; he toiled, slaved, sweated over his manuscript; his style is not in the least spontaneous, but rather the result of elaborate ingenuity, with more than a dash of downright perversity. It is contagious, too, as is shown in some of the estimates written of him by his admirers. His style is not only bad for a novel, it is bad anyway, it contains passages that perplex and torture, rather than interest or inspire. Take this sentence from *Lord Ormont and His Aminta*:

Was she not colour the sight of men?

Meredith was a Master-Mind, but not a Master of English Prose; a master is like a fine man on a fine horse, you admire both the controller and the controlled.

Meredith's true vein might have been poetic drama. He was born at the wrong time. If he had only been an Elizabethan, or had belonged to the latter half of the twentieth century! He had great dramatic qualities, wonderful idyllic powers, was full of blood, and always a poet at heart. His splendid intellectual endowments would have made him a worthy contemporary of Marlowe and Chapman, and in that open-air age he would probably have written masterpieces for the stage. He is not quite a great lyric poet, nor a great novelist; poetic drama would have allowed his genius to become more articulate. It is highly significant of the domination of the Novel that this man should have elected to write in that form; also a great compliment to the Novel.

George Meredith was not so complete a Pagan as Thomas Hardy, but he was essentially Pagan; his real emphasis is on this life and on this present world; he speaks vaguely of God, but the Divine Power has no important rôle in his books, either as an immanent force or as our Father in Heaven. His men and women get along somehow without religion, and fight their own battles without looking up. Yet Hardy is an avowed pessimist, and Meredith's novels always give the impression of optimism. With no premises but the external world and its history to work from, Hardy reaches pessimism and Meredith optimism. This latter conclusion is perhaps owing to two factors.

First, Meredith was hearty, robust, genial, buoyant; his men and women delight in violent exercise, eat copious meals, and rejoice in old wine; they find the world jovial, and add to its joviality. Hardy, on the other hand, while tenderly sympathetic, and delicately responsive, has little geniality. He watches people feasting, but cannot feast himself; he is sorry for them, feeling sure that tears will follow laughter. If he ultimately reaches heaven, as through his sincerity and tenderness he ought to, his occupation will be gone, for there both sympathy and lamentation should be superfluous.

Second, Meredith believed (at least artistically) that men and women are not passive instruments of Fate; he thought that men and women can conquer heredity, environment, yes, fate itself; his stout-hearted heroes and heroines are at all times masters of their own destiny. The fault, dear Brutus, is not in our stars, but in ourselves, that we are underlings. In Hardy's eyes, we are mere bits of the vast machine; we have no more influence than the spoke of a fly-wheel; we do not have to wait until we are dead before we are rolled round with rocks, and stones, and trees.

Thomas Hardy's superiority as a novelist over Meredith consists mainly in three things: the perfection of constructive power (no novelist was ever a better architect), the beautiful stately march of his style (first chapter of *Return of the Native*, or Gabriel Oak telling time by the stars), and the universal character of his *dramatis personæ*. For, after all, Meredith deals merely with interesting groups of people, only occasionally, as in Clara Middleton, showing the type; while all Hardy's folk have the touch of nature. They interest us not because of their individuality, but because they are so poignantly human.

On the second of July, 1905, Meredith wrote in a letter to a friend, ''Hardy was here some days back. I am always glad to see him, and have regrets at his going; for the double reason, that I like him, and am afflicted by his twilight view of life.'' And one can hardly conceive of Mr. Hardy writing so jovial a letter as this, written when Meredith was about forty years old. ''I am every morning on the top of Box Hill—as its flower, its bird, its prophet. I drop down the moon on one side, I draw up the sun on t'other. I breathe fine air. I shout ha ha to the gates of the world. Then I descend and know myself a donkey for doing it.'' The last sentence betrays the Englishman.

Meredith had the modern contempt for asceticism. In a letter to the Rev. Dr. Jessopp, he said, ''Can I morally admire, or reverence, or see positive virtue in St. Simeon? Was he a hero, of his kind? Does the contemplation of him bring us nearer to God? To what a God! I turn aching in all my flesh to adore the Pagan, in preference. . . . Don't you see that it is not adoration moves the stinking Saint, but, basest

of prostrations, Terror. . . . Be not misled by
this dirty piece of picturesque Religiosity, ani-
mated: my gorge rises! I hold my nostrils. I
cry for a Southwest wind to arise.''

As a final word on Meredith's religion, it is
well to cite what he wrote about prayer, in a
long letter to his son. ''Look for the truth in
everything, and follow it, and you will then be
living justly before God.   Let nothing flout your
sense of a Supreme Being, and be certain that
your understanding wavers whenever you
chance to doubt that he leads to good.   We grow
to good as surely as the plant grows to the light.
The school has only to look through history for
a scientific assurance of it.   And do not lose
the habit of praying to the unseen Divinity.
Prayer for worldly goods is worse than fruitless, but prayer for strength of soul is that
passion of the soul which catches the gift it
seeks.''

Over and over again he points out the eternal
consequences of acts.   In *Rhoda Fleming,* he
says that we are immortal not in what we are,
but in what we do; our acts go on forever, and

it is only fools who think they can do anything and somehow avoid the consequences.

We feel certain that Meredith was a Theorist, a Philosopher, a Moralist, and a Teacher. But it is impossible to say exactly what his theory of life was, whither his philosophy led him, on what his system of ethics was founded, and precisely what it is he teaches. Dickens represents Sin as something repulsive and malignant, and sinners as malicious; look at Quilp. Meredith represents sin as Folly, and sinners as Fools. Sir Willoughby is an ass; the two young men in *Rhoda Fleming* are fools; the one who repents seems simply to become sane; the other remains a fool, a fool positive. When the husband of her friend tries to put his arm around Diana's waist, he is represented as not so criminal as silly, and he is forgiven. To be sure, the attempt is the only kind of compliment some men know how to pay a woman.

Meredith's hatred of asceticism and conventional standards led him in his later work near the borders of the rather dangerous doctrine that the instincts of the heart are superior to the statute-book. We must trust nature, he seems to say, which is, of course, pagan rather than Christian doctrine. Meredith did not believe with Jeremiah and Browning in the deceitfulness and corruption of man's heart. Clara is absolutely right in breaking the engagement; Diana was right in cultivating an intimacy with an outsider; and in *Lord Ormont,* the final step is taken: Aminta leaves her husband, simply because she loves another man.

A contemporary reviewer (1894) said of this book that the exposition and the story were easily detachable. The story is pretty and almost to the end, natural. The exposition is worthless. One hardened critic said he felt very uncomfortable in reading the book because "Aminta had no case that could be granted in a Sioux City divorce court." Now do we admire Thackeray less, or more, because he refused to yield to his passion for Mrs. Brookfield?

Not only did Meredith glorify the instincts of the heart at the expense of law and order, he glorified the liberty of the individual above all discipline. He himself had an undisciplined mind, and hated system; what would he have thought of Germany to-day? Consider his attitude toward the boy Crossjay in the *Egoist,* and think what the "system" did to Richard Feverel. In attempting to create our sympathy for Diana after her crooked transaction, he made not only a moral but an artistic error, and was partially aware of it, for in a letter written in 1884, he said, "Diana of the Crossways keeps me still on her sad last way to wedlock. I could have killed her merrily, with my compliments to the public; and that was my intention."

Meredith is the most chivalrous of novelists, and women ought to be fond of him. He loved Diana, even though he made her sell the news; and he will not forgive her fiancé because the latter will not forgive her. Redworth is the real lover; he loves Diana, not her attributes. After all, we don't love people for their qualities, but for themselves. Meredith believed ardently in woman suffrage, and though he counselled the militants against violence, it was clear that he sympathised with them. He said they must have patience and not think that John Bull will move for a solitary kick. His attitude toward Diana, Lucy, Rhoda and Aminta affords sufficient illustration of his chivalrous love of women.

Akin to this feeling—and as un-English as his love of France—was his appreciation and glorification of the Irish. He loved the Celtic race with all his heart. His Irish characters illuminate his pages; they shine in strong and intentional contrast with the stolid Englishmen. I think he loved them mainly for their chivalrous lack of prudence, for their dash and recklessness. In *Diana,* we find the following observation: "English women and men feel toward the quick-witted of their species as to aliens, having the demerits of aliens—wordiness, vanity, obscurity, shallowness, an empty glitter, the sin of posturing."

Those who have never read anything of Meredith, which includes the vast majority of the earth's inhabitants, ought to begin with *Rhoda Fleming*. It is not only the most normal in style of all his compositions, it is in many ways the most powerfully dramatic. The conflict here is between natures that do not and cannot understand one another; natures whose hearts break, but cannot bend. Besides the leading actors, an indelible impression is left on the reader's mind by the farmhand Gammon. In a house black with awful tragedy, this clod eats prodigious meals with undiminished appetite, and thus exerts a wholesome influence on all the inmates; unconsciously he is a philosopher, showing both the importunate necessity, and the healing power, of food and sleep. It is plain that Meredith is in hearty sympathy with him.

The characters in Meredith's novels are not as a rule abnormal or indeed unusual; they are presented to the reader in an abnormal and unusual manner. He dresses them up in astonishing motley; could we strip their souls bare, they would be just like other folks. It is the same with his incidents; he uses an extraordinary style to describe ordinary events.

In the *Egoist*, what kind of a girl was Clara? Simply a "very nice girl." Her chief claim to our admiration is her personal beauty. There is nothing remarkable about her mind or temperament, and she might easily be found in a novel by Robert W. Chambers. The distance between Mr. Chambers and Meredith is in the expense of energy. Clara is normal, like the young girls in our popular American writer; but Meredith uses all the artillery of his mind in bombarding the reader with presentations, introductions, comments, so that we finally take in Clara from every conceivable angle.

Like most thoughtful men, Meredith was impressed with the devouring selfishness of the ordinary male. This is brought out in one of the earliest and perhaps the greatest of his novels, *The Ordeal of Richard Feverel,* where the heroine is illogically killed in order to emphasise the text. In the *Egoist,* of course, we have a powerful, minute, and prolonged analysis of the one unpardonable sin. Sir Willoughby is a blighting and ubiquitous curse; and the most cruel moment for him is when at last there crosses his brain the shadow of a doubt of his own perfection.

I remember Meredith for certain scenes rather than for certain books; it may be a damaging admission, but I have never wished a single one of his novels to be longer, and am usually heartily glad when I come to the end. For all his display of fireworks, I find myself forgetting his plots, forgetting his characters; I remember the horsewhip in *Beauchamp's Career* more vividly than any of the men or women, and I should dislike to humiliate any of my friends by asking them pointblank to give an accurate résumé of the story. The idyllic river scene in *Richard Feverel,* the parting of Richard and Lucy—these stay bright in the memory.

I am certain that Meredith's style gets between the reader and the characters like a hedge; at times it is completely opaque. He was too much in love with his phrases, and must have thought them better than they really are. For although it is blasphemous to say so, I regard the aphorisms in *Richard Feverel* as inferior to the aphorisms in *Pudd'nhead Wilson.*

Meredith himself was a thousand times more interesting than any of his works. The best part of all his stories is where he shows us most of himself. It is vain to classify him, to call him realist or romanticist. The marine duet in *Lord Ormont* is pure romanticism, but the election scenes in *Beauchamp* are pure realism. As a rule, however, Meredith never shows us *our* world, as Jane Austen does, he gives us tantalising, fragmentary glimpses of *his* world.

Meredith and Browning were alike in their tremendous masculinity, in their pre-occupation with the passion of love, and in their capacity for profound introspection. No intelligent reader of literature can fail to notice the points of similarity. Oscar Wilde summed them up ironically by saying, "Meredith is a prose Browning; and so is Browning."

With Tennyson—both in his art and in his viewpoint—Meredith had nothing in common. The delicacy and conventionality of *The Idylls of the King* infuriated Meredith. "The *Holy Grail* is wonderful, isn't it? The lines are satin lengths, the figures Sèvres china. I have not the courage to offer to review it. I should say such things. To think!—it's in these days that

the foremost poet of the country goes on fluting
of creatures that have not a breath of vital humanity in them . . . to hear the chorus of
praise too! Why, this stuff is not the Muse, it's
Musery. . . . I read the successive mannered
lines with pain—yards of linen-drapery for the
delight of ladies who would be in the fashion."

Shortly before his death, Meredith unwill-
ingly attempted to appraise his novels. In this
fashion he spoke: "I have not made any esti-
mate of the value of my books in prose. . . .
The *Egoist* comes nearer than the other books
to the proper degree of roundness and finish.
In *Diana of the Crossways* my critics own that
a breathing woman is produced, and I felt that
she was in me as I wrote. *Rhoda Fleming* is
liked by some, not much by me. *Richard Feverel* was earnestly conceived, and is in some
points worthy of thought. *Beauchamp's Career* does not probe so deeply, but is better work
on the surface.—I have treated my books of
prose as the mother bird her fledgelings."

Perhaps the best thing he ever said of his
own work occurs in his novel *Beauchamp's Ca-*

reer, although being in a novel, instead of in a private letter, the style of saying it is too consciously elaborate. "Those happy tales of mystery are as much my envy as the popular narratives of the deeds of bread and cheese people, for they both create a tideway in the attentive mind; the mysterious pricking our credulous flesh to creep, the familiar urging our obese imagination to constitutional exercise. And oh, the refreshment there is in dealing with characters either contemptibly beneath us, or supernaturally above! My way is like a Rhone island in the summer drought, stony, unattractive and difficult between the two forceful streams of the unreal and the over-real, which delight mankind—honour to the conjurers! My people conquer nothing, win none; they are actual, yet uncommon. It is the clockwork of the brain that they are directed to set in motion, and—poor troop of actors to empty benches!—the conscience residing in thoughtfulness which they would appeal to; and if you are there impervious to them, we are lost; back I go to my wilderness, where, as you perceive, I have contracted the habit of listening to my own voice more than is good.''

Meredith was a fantastic genius, often reaching the sublime, often the absurd. The "leg" business in *The Egoist* is irritatingly ridiculous, and could hardly have been survived by a lesser man; his conversations often become fantastical, and he leads us to heights where we breathe rarefied air, rather than the invigorating breeze of the uplands. His pictures of Nature are sometimes glorious, sometimes abominably overdone. The school scene with which *Lord Ormont* closes is fantastical, and amid the dialogue and incidents of *The Amazing Marriage* the reader moves in a luminous mist.

If we live long enough, it will be interesting to watch the oscillations of Meredith's reputation, and to see where he finally comes to rest. One irate journalist wrote of him some twenty years ago, "The public which so long neglected him was right. The public which now reads him is a conscientious public. It has been taught to think it likes him, or ought to like him. It does not like him; and the wave of incomplete

popularity, swollen by adroit advertising, will
presently spend its force and leave Mr. Meredith permanently stranded on a desolate shore.''

Well, he is still afloat, despite the storms of
time and the torpedoes of critics.   If he remains
on the ocean of literature, it will be because his
natural genius was so great and his own mind
so interesting that there will always be a select
class of experienced travellers who will enjoy
voyages in his company.

We in America, who have always liked him
better and understood him more sympathetically
than his own countrymen, ought to remember
him with pleasure, because he spoke so warmly
of us.   In a letter written in 1886, he said,
''Americans appear to have received my work
very generously.   Since their most noble clos-
ing of the Civil War, I have looked to them as
the hope of our civilisation. . . . Therefore I
am justly flattered by their praise, if I win it;
their censure, if they deal it to me, I meditate
on.''

Just three months before his death, he wrote,
''The English, unlike the Americans, have not

accepted me in the form of a poet. I had to pay for the publication of my books of verse. Indeed, the run of the novels started from American appreciation.''

Of the bright array of eminent Victorian British novelists, only one remains alive— Thomas Hardy. He is three-quarters of a century old, but it is not the dignity of age that gives him his present commanding position in literature; it is the simple fact that of all living English novelists, none can possibly be considered his rival. We may indeed truthfully omit the word English; there is no writer in the world to-day whose prose fiction is of equal value. His first novel was published in 1871, and then for twenty-five years his works appeared with no real pause.

With a third of his life he seems to have achieved immortality. What has he done with the other two-thirds? Grown up, practised architecture, written much verse, and for the last twenty years appeared before the public as a professional poet and historical dramatist.

Granville Barker had the audacity to put *The Dynasts* on the stage. His next attempt will perhaps be the *Encyclopædia Britannica*.

Mr. Hardy's mind is so interesting, so richly meditative, so pregnant in fancy, and his view of art so architecturally orderly, that anything and everything he writes has both value and charm; but I regard these last twenty years sadly, as I think what might have been; just as I regret the twenty years that Milton spent in politics, and as I rejoice over Goethe's refusal to do so, or even to become "patriotic." Genius is the scarcest thing on earth except radium; and to see it wasted is like being adrift in an open boat and watching some one wasting fresh water.

Mr. Hardy has written fifteen novels: ten are works of genius. I except *Desperate Remedies* because of its immaturity; *The Hand of Ethelberta* because of its triviality; *The Romantic Adventures of a Milkmaid* because of its slenderness in content; *Jude the Obscure* because of its hysterical exaggeration; *The Well-Beloved* because of its unreality. There remain ten great contributions to English fiction, ten great novels, a few of which, like *The Return of the Native, Far from the Madding Crowd,* and *Tess,* are established classics in literature, so far as we of to-day can see. And a person who should like *The Woodlanders* best of all—though I do not, preferring *The Return of the Native*—would have no need to apologise.

Mr. Hardy adhered to the old Victorian tradition in publishing his novels serially. Of the fifteen novels, twelve appeared in successive instalments in periodicals. In fact, only the first two originally appeared in book form. Has this method had anything to do with the author's skill in holding his reader in suspense? Perhaps not; though it is well to remember the fact in studying the construction of *Far From the Madding Crowd.* True it is, that although Mr. Hardy's novels are full of solidly satisfying qualities, not even Conan Doyle or Phillips Oppenheim has any more power in compelling the reader to turn the next page. The difference is that if one tells you in advance the outcome of a story by these lesser worthies, your interest is

dead; who reads Oppenheim twice? Whereas
Mr. Hardy's books gain in excitement every
time I read them, and there is only one where
a knowledge of the conclusion subtracts much
from the interest—*A Laodicean;* that book is
different from all the rest of the work of its
author, and was written under peculiar circumstances.

Mr. Hardy is just beginning to be known in
France; I think he will eventually conquer the
Continent. Although his subjects are insular,
his style is not, and his thoughts wander through
eternity. Mr. Hardy writes as though he lived
on another planet, and by means of some tremendous astronomical contrivance, were able
to see earth's inhabitants life-size, and regard
them with the exclusive attention of a student,
himself entirely remote from their concerns.
He feels as the astronomer of the Lick observa-
tory felt, when he turned the mighty telescope
on flaming San Francisco; he breathed the keen,
cool air of the mountain-top; but brought close
within his vision were some hundreds of thousands of people living in hell. The astronomer's

heart was wrung with pity at the spectacle; pity and horror; but there was nothing he could do, except continue to look. Man's extremity is Mr. Hardy's opportunity; but it is an opportunity only for art. Pessimism will help us all, he believes, by taking forever away illusory hopes which fade into anguish; those who expect nothing cannot be disappointed. The façade of a prison, he thinks, is more cheerful to contemplate than the façade of a palace. At any rate we know it to be a prison, and enter it with submissive despair; much better so than to have it resemble a palace outside.

CHAPTER VIII

CONRAD, GALSWORTHY AND OTHERS

The triple combination in Joseph Conrad—his lack of popularity—not a refractor, but a reflector—his tales of the sea—his silent women—ethical value of his work—John Galsworthy—a satirist—his hatred of British hypocrisy—his mistake in *The Dark Flower*—J. M. Barrie—the contrast between *Sentimental Tommy* and *Tommy and Grizzel* —May Sinclair—Mary Willcocks.

MANY years ago, when I read for the first time *The Constitutional History of the United States,* written by a gentleman in the Black Forest called Hermann von Holst, I was impressed by his prefatory remark (in English) that whereas there had been many histories of the United States, none had equalled this in soberness of mind. Although it might have sounded better if some one else had said it, the remark was instructive, and serves to separate sheep from goats in modern novels. What contemporary English novelists write with soberness of mind? Surely not Hall Caine, or Conan Doyle, or Flor-

ence Barclay, or Robert Hichens. Mr. Wells and Mr. Bennett? Sometimes, but not all the time. Thomas Hardy, always; and with equal soberness, though not with equal felicity, Joseph Conrad, J. M. Barrie, John Galsworthy, Miss Sinclair, and Miss Willcocks. No modern novelists have higher ideals than these five.

The ability to write for publication in a language other than one's mother-tongue is not altogether unknown; as is shown by the instances of Turgenev, Maarten Maartens, Oscar Wilde, and Rabindranath Tagore. But the case of Joseph Conrad is unique. He knew no English at all until he was nineteen, and it was not until his thirty-eighth year that he published anything. When he determined to become an author, his perplexity was quite unlike the obstacle that balks most writers. The question that Mr. Conrad put to himself was, *"In what language shall I write?"* Now that is not the question that troubles the mind of most men of letters. The question that afflicts their peace is not, In what language shall I write, but What shall I say? I have read a great many novels, and it is plain that in the majority of cases this latter is the paramount issue.

Mr. Conrad's mother-tongue is, of course, Polish; but although he had before him the example of Sienkiewicz, there was to be nothing of Poland in the books to be written, and every reason why he should make a direct appeal to a wider audience than could possibly be found among his countrymen. His first intention was to write in French, a language he had known from childhood; this impulse was strengthened by the fact that he was deeply read in French fiction, and really learned the novelist's art from French masters. He has a keen admiration for Flaubert and De Maupassant; and has successfully imitated their calm, deliberate, impersonal style. But he had sailed many years under an English flag; he knew he must write stories of the sea; his closest friends were all English; and he loved the vigour of the English tongue. His experiences as transmuted into fiction would appeal to Anglo-Saxons more than to any other people; and these causes combined placed him in English literature. It is a great compliment to our language that so thoughtful and ambitious a man should select it out of a possible three.

Teodor Jozef Konrad Korzeniovski was born in the south of Poland, on the sixth of December, 1857.   He had splendid intellectual ancestry.   For generations his family had been men of fine mental powers, and, what is much rarer among the Slavs, of great practical vigour and resolution.   His father was a revolutionist in 1862, and was imprisoned, dying in 1870.   His mother was exiled to Siberia, and died in 1865. At the age of twelve he had thus lost both his parents, and perhaps began then to develop that calm self-reliance so peculiarly characteristic of him.   As a lad, he longed to get away from inland Poland and see the ends of the earth; he particularly had to a high degree what every healthy boy has in some measure—the passion of the sea.   In his stories *Heart of Darkness* and *Youth,* there are many autobiographical passages illustrative of his wanderlust.

It was in 1878 that he first saw England.   He settled in Lowestoft (shades of Dickens!) and scraped acquaintance with all kinds of fishers and sea-faring men. He shipped on board a coasting-vessel, kept his observant eyes open, studied English, studied navigation, and after some time secured a mate's certificate. Then he made his first voyage to the East, the effect of which on his sensitive mind is shown in *Youth;* this story exhibits his intellectual eagerness and the vivid impression made by an exotic world on his fresh young heart.

For nearly twenty years he was a sailor-man, in the good old times before the supremacy of steam. During the long days out of sight of land he was constantly and unconsciously collecting material for his novels. During the long watches of the night his profound and introspective Slav mind meditated deeply, turning over and over thoughts that were some day to appear on the printed page. For even in the most objective of Conrad's books, there is always the reflective cast. His only attempts at composition were to be found in the log-book, and in occasional letters to his kin in Poland.

Once John Galsworthy was a passenger. If

gossip be true, the Englishman's attention was attracted to the ship's officer by the latter's loud and fluent and picturesque profanity; all of which he must have used up at sea, for there is almost no swearing in his books. At all events, the two men became intimate friends, and have something higher than admiration for each other's art.

In 1894—great year of modern fiction— Mr. Conrad quit the sea, and looked over the completed manuscript of *Almayer's Folly,* which he had begun some years before. He took lodgings in London and determined to spend six months in absolute laziness, for, as he expresses it, "he was seized, suddenly and inexplicably, by a desire to rest." He had dropped his last Polish name, for it is not pleasant even to men less sensitive than Conrad to hear their own family appellation invariably mispronounced.

In 1895 appeared his first novel, and since that time the history of his life is the history of his publications, novel following novel at regular and decent intervals. No living man is better qualified for the literary profession. His many years of active life, going down to the sea in ships, have stocked his mind with a superabundance of dramatic material; his wide reading in three modern literatures has taught him much about the art of composition; his sharply sensitive and profoundly reflective Slav temperament has given to his observations and reflections a quaintly original flavour. His face to some extent is a map of his soul. He looks like a competent, fearless, and highly intelligent clipper captain. His eyes have looked on the brutality of nature and the brutality of man, and are unafraid. It is not an adventurous face; it has nothing of George Meredith's recklessness. It is a face that knows the worst of the ocean and the worst of the heart of man, and while taking no risks, realising all dangers, is calmly, pessimistically resolute. This is not the man to lead a forlorn hope, but unquestionably the man to leave in charge; grave, steady, reliable.

Apart from his seamanship, he has a really extraordinary endowment and equipment as a novelist. A Slav by birth, a Frenchman in training, an Anglo-Saxon in activity! His Slavonic genius is shown in the skill with which he has acquired the English language; temperamentally, it is shown in his aloofness; his lack of prejudice; his sincerity, dignity, and truthfulness. The most Slavonic of all his novels is, of course, *Under Western Eyes,* reminiscent of Dostoevski; but the temperament appears in them all, with the possible exception of *Victory,* a novel quite unworthy of him, and which he has apparently tried to write in a manner not his own.

His mastery of English is marvellous, because his chief glory is perhaps his style, something that only Stevenson has combined with sea-fiction. Smollett, Scott, Cooper, Marryat, Russell, all distinguished in tales of the ocean, have no particular rhetorical merit. And Jack London is really an amateur sailor. Like all great English writers, Conrad has studied with assiduity the English Bible. There are not many of its phrases in his books, but its influence is there.

Conrad is the heir of Stevenson. Stevenson

died in December, 1894, and the very next year appeared Conrad's first novel. It is as though Stevenson's soul had migrated to the new man. How Stevenson would have enjoyed reading *Typhoon* or *The Nigger of the Narcissus,* and what wonderful letters he would have written to Mr. Archer and Mr. Colvin! In 1895 Kipling was in the zenith of his glory, and his tales of the East were inspiring the West. Here was Conrad's opportunity. Stevenson and Kipling, however, were, as they have been rightly called, "observant landsmen"; mere reporters of the deep. Joseph Conrad and Pierre Loti are sea-dogs and artists. And Conrad is more sincere than Loti; he has the Slavonic calmness and clearness of vision. The Frenchman is elaborate, ornamental; indeed, with all his virtues, Pierre Loti is a *poseur,* whether he is talking about the sea or about religion; and he has no reticence. Conrad is more silent, more grave, but just as sensitive as the picturesque Frenchman.

Conrad has never been a popular writer, and a large number of intelligent and well-read per-

sons have never heard his name. His books
have not synchronised with public taste. He
began his literary career at just the moment
when the new Romanticism was fashionable,
when every one was reading *The Prisoner of
Zenda* and *A Gentleman of France*. Now there
is nothing romantic about Conrad except his
medium—the sea. At present he is writing in
the flood-tide of the biographical novel, something utterly foreign to his manner as thus far
displayed. He is the psychologist of sailors;
a kind of union of Richardson and Smollett;
and there is no place for him except what he can
make for himself. Yet, although he has no
public, he has great fame—his case being analogous to that of George Meredith and Henry
James. No living writer has been more highly
praised by men whose praise is worth having.
The verdict of thoughtful and high-standard
critics is practically unanimous. Many cita-
tions might be made, most of which would seem
extravagant; we have space only for one, that
written by John Galsworthy in the *Fortnightly
Review* in 1908. Mentioning the list of Con-

rad's novels from 1896 to 1908, Mr. Galsworthy remarked, "The writing of these ten books is probably the only writing of the last twelve years that will enrich the English language to any great extent." He calls his friend "a seer," and says he has the "cosmic spirit."

Mr. Conrad himself comments, "Praise and blame to my mind are of singularly small import, yet one cares for the recognition of a certain ampleness of purpose." If Mr. Conrad means he does not care whether he is praised or blamed, I do not believe him; but all he actually says here is that he wishes to be taken seriously. He need have no misgivings; his most thoughtful admirers take him seriously, and the great bulk of readers take him so seriously that they refuse to take him at all. One critic calls the circle of his readers "inexplicably small." There is nothing inexplicable about it. A good many years ago some one said of Browning that he had done less to conciliate and more to influence the public than any other man of his time. Conrad has no more amenity than Browning. Stevenson passed joyously from incident to inci-

dent; Conrad holds one incident before our eyes,
analysing it, reflecting upon it, describing it—
like a lecturer who talks about something that
interests him rather than his audience. Conrad is over-careful for popular taste; over-careful in minuteness and accuracy of description,
over-careful in analysis, over-careful in the
shades of his conversations. And his method
of construction, shown at its worst in *Chance,*
is irritating to all readers, and to some, maddening. No, the wonder is not that Conrad's
readers are so few; the wonder is that they are
not fewer. That they are steadily increasing
in number is one more evidence of the standards
of taste.

Artists who write to please themselves—that
is, to satisfy the imperious demands of their conscience—are more happy, I must believe, than
the successful caterers to the public. The man
who writes novels to please the public is like an
actor, a singer, a parlour entertainer; his happiness has passed beyond his control, and is in
the keeping of others. A slight diminution in
applause casts a shadow on his heart. Some-

times we hear the absurd remark that actors must be tired of coming before the curtain at the tenth or eleventh recall. Why, that is the very breath of life to them! Indifference or perfunctory applause destroys their happiness; and they are entirely at the mercy of the caprice of the public. But a serious artist, who does his best all the time, even with scant recognition, enjoys the pure delight of creation; lack of wide recognition cannot make him unhappy, for the sources of his pleasure are elsewhere; and when, at the end, fame comes to him, as it is bound to come, if he really be a genius, then he has the pleasure of gaining the whole world and saving his own soul.

Admirable writer as he is, Conrad can never rank with the great Slav novelists, Tolstoi, Turgenev, Dostoevski. For not only does he lack the universality of these men, his style—probably because he writes in an alien tongue—lacks the transparent quality of the Slav masters. The style of Tolstoi and Turgenev is like plate glass; you do not know whether it is there or not, you are so interested in what it reveals, so little aware of the medium of revelation. Now Conrad's well-wrought style is highly self-conscious; it is never a happy accident. He is a most deliberate artist, and has not only pondered deeply about his art, but has not hesitated to write about it. He is, as might be expected, an intense admirer of Henry James, an author who should be offered only to foreign students of the most advanced grades. He calls Mr. James "a great artist," and agrees with him that Fiction is nearer truth than History. History takes documents as a base; fiction, men and women. Both men insist on the dignity of the novel. The artist is the interpreter. Some one has said we cannot understand Romanised Britain because no artists survive who might have interpreted it to us; Rome, at the same period, we know pretty well.

Mr. Conrad, in speaking of what is perhaps his masterpiece, *The Nigger of the Narcissus* (1897), says, "It is the book by which, not as a novelist perhaps, but as an artist striving for the utmost sincerity of expression, I am willing to stand or fall." Even at that early stage of his career he wrote a preface to his book (suppressed on advice), which would sound pretentious were it not so flamingly sincere; and which gives his artistic creed, a statement of belief to which he has always firmly adhered. Every reader of Conrad's stories should study this preface; and one passage should be quoted here. "The artist appeals to that part of our being which is not dependent on wisdom; to that in us which is a gift and not an acquisition—and, therefore, more permanently enduring. He speaks to our capacity for delight and wonder, to the sense of mystery surrounding our lives: to our sense of pity, and beauty, and pain: to the latent feeling of fellowship with all creation —and to the subtle but invincible conviction of solidarity that knits together the loneliness of innumerable hearts to the solidarity in dreams, in joy, in sorrow, in aspirations, in illusions, in hope, in fear, which binds men to each other, which binds together all humanity—the dead to the living and the living to the unborn."

This preface might have been written by Fielding to *Tom Jones,* except for one phrase,

"the sense of mystery surrounding our lives";
for that sense of mystery does not appear in
eighteenth century fiction, and its total absence
from *Tom Jones* prevents that novel from being
the best novel in the English language. The
novel has advanced since 1749.

Conrad stands alone in modern fiction, belonging to no school, and under the influence of
no group. He has a praiseworthy impatience
with dogmas like Realism, Sentimentalism,
Naturalism, Romanticism, saying, "Liberty of
the imagination is the most precious possession
of a novelist." He insists, too, that no matter
how objective a novelist may be, he never describes the world—he describes his own world,
the world as he sees it. And in order to describe even this subjective world, he must rid
himself not only of artistic dogmas, but philosophical ones, like pessimism and optimism.
Optimism may seem jauntily shallow, but pessimism, says Mr. Conrad, is intellectual arro-
gance. Consistent pessimists are certainly, I
think, rarer than consistent optimists. Mr.
Conrad says that every attempt to explain this

universe ethically is a failure; but, to use his
phrase, it is a "spectacular" universe, full of
wonder, mystery, delight—above all, interesting. Thus those realists who attempt to represent life as dully monotonous would seem to be
barred by Conrad from the ranks of true novelists. For my part, however dull life at times
may be, I have never found life, even in its grey-
est moments, so dull as many books that profess
to describe it.

Those that have not yet surrendered to Conrad, and many there be that are offended in
him,—and also those who have not read him at
all, should read first, *Typhoon* and then *The
Nigger of the Narcissus*. Conrad's stories of
the East sound to me—who have never been
there, and am quite willing to see it through better eyes than my own—more truthful than Kipling's. The latter is a born exaggerator, incapable of moderation—witness his remarks in the
present war—Conrad is more cool, more aloof.
Like his famous Captain in *Typhoon*, Conrad
describes fearful storms in nature and frightful

passions in man, with an extraordinary poise—
the calm of the observant artist.

The literature of all nations is filled with descriptions of the wrath of the ocean; thousands
of writers have done their best to reproduce in
the mind of the reader the sublime and terrible
spectacle. But I do not think I have read anywhere a more real account than in *Typhoon;* one
feels engulfed, like the two men on the bridge.
Yet the originality and power of this wonderful
story do not lie mainly in the pictures of the
storm; the true interest is in the struggle between the hideous forces of nature at their
worst, and the skill of one man. Captain Mac-
Whirr is the only person who can beat the sea.
He conquers the ocean, because he has no more
imagination than the ocean, really no more sen-
tient life than the ocean. Nature is ruthless,
unconscious, unaware; but so is Captain Mac-
Whirr. And in this Captain, nature meets her
master, because joined with equal unconscious-
ness is the power of intention; definite purpose.
He is there to save his ship, and he intends to

save it. His quelling the riot on board with the
same inflexible discipline that he would have observed on a calm night illustrates his character.
Conrad has shown us clearly what manner of
man he is in the extraordinary incident of the
change of flags; and now in the tempest his very
inertia wears out the patience of the storm.
Had he possessed one spark of self-conscious-
ness, one flash of imagination, his ship would
have been lost. He has the invincible courage
that goes with essentially stupid minds; he has
no fear because the possibility of choice does
not even occur to him. Captain MacWhirr is
as stupid as Destiny itself; and in this adventure seems to defeat Destiny.

In *The Nigger of the Narcissus,* and if I
could have only one of Conrad's books, I would
take this one, Conrad shows his profound sympathy with the children of the forecastle. I
wonder if he exhibited as much sympathy with
them when he was in active command as he does
in the pages of this book? This is a real "sea-
story," with appropriate incidents, but differ-
entiated from its class by profound and subtle

psychological analysis. To see what mere
thoughtfulness has done to the art of fiction, it
is instructive to compare Cooper's Long Tom
Coffin in *The Pilot* with old Singleton in this
narrative. It is the difference between childhood and maturity. Sea-fiction has "grown
up," has become deeply reflective as well as de-
scriptive, is taking itself earnestly. Conrad
would not write like Cooper if he could; and
Cooper could not have written like Conrad, because between the two came the whole Victorian age of serious thought. This is a tale of the
sea, written by one who loved it, who loved it
with exaggerated intensity in the safe glow of
reminiscence; but it is written with soberness
of mind, with the intent to reveal the very heart
of human mystery.

Although Conrad denounces pessimism, most
of his stories are deeply tragic, are full of the
sickness of heart that comes from deferred
hopes, full of frustration and despair. He ex-
cels particularly in the depiction of remorse.
Prometheus was comfortable compared to these
men and women of Conrad, whose hearts are

torn by the vulture of memory. His tragedies usually happen in far-off places, India or Africa —or they happen to obscure and unimportant people in big western cities. His first book, *Almayer's Folly,* is an illustration of the first, *The Secret Agent* of the second. No imaginative reader can possibly forget the awful scene toward the close of Almayer, where the man carefully obliterates the traces of the girl's footsteps.

Conrad's women are highly interesting, although unlike any women I have ever met. They have an endless capacity for suffering with no power of articulation. Most women that I have known suffer less and talk more. There is something hideous in the dumb pain of these creatures. They open not their mouths. In the story of Falk, the awful remorse of the man who has eaten a human body is confronted with the stolid silent suffering of the passionate woman who loves him. In *The Secret Agent,* the woman is in hell all the time; but no one can get a word out of her. In *Chance,* it is plain that the young girl is not happy; yet every attempt to elicit from her any speech that shall give a key to her pain so that it can be relieved, is fruitless; all that a friend can do is to adopt a policy of watchful waiting, successful in this instance as it catches the young lady in the quiet but determined effort at suicide. These passive, undemonstrative, silent women have a reticence that is maddening; one feels that if they were physically ill, the greatest diagnostician in the world could make nothing of them; would have to resort to the wildest guesses. We all of us know persons who are undemonstrative, though they are sufficiently rare to seem eccentric; but where has Conrad met these women who are totally unresponsive? who greet small-talk, threats, curses, honest enquiry, and affectionate solicitude with nothing but steadfast eyes, in which the fires of the pit are smouldering? I had rather dwell on the housetop with a contentious woman in a continual dropping of water than with one of these creatures who look so significant and never by any chance say anything.

Conrad himself as a novelist is taciturn, exceedingly chary of comment. Compare him with a garrulous artist like Thackeray, who chatters at his helpless reader with the fluency of a barber! Conrad is unlike the English novelists in his silent gravity, and he is totally unlike the Germans in his brevity and lack of sentiment. He points out to us the wonder of the sea, but he indulges in no rhapsodies thereupon; he shows us the variety of human nature in one forecastle, with no moralising and no gush— merely an occasional query, as, why do those sailors read only Bulwer-Lytton?

Conrad is not always easy reading; partly because of his solidity of phrase, partly because of his peculiar method, illustrated at its extreme in *Chance*. He wishes to get the vital effect of the first person talking without making the chief character speak. Thus we have the interposition of Marlow, who is a good deal of a bore. The reader is four removes from Conrad's mind. We get at the characters and the events of the story through what some one has said to some one else, who is a friend of Marlow's, who in turn reports to us. This gives

Conrad full opportunity to show his characters in all kinds of reflected lights, and from all manner of angles; but it is sometimes perplexing. The fact is that while Dickens is a refracting telescope, Conrad is a reflector. Dickens turns the lens of his powerful imagination directly on individuals like Micawber or Dick Swiveller, and with their qualities magnified, and brought close to the reader, we see them in a strong light and they become hugely interesting. Conrad does not have us look directly at the object, but rather at a mirror in which the object is reflected. This mirror may be simply the effect produced on some other person or persons by the leading character, or it may be simply the clear surface of Marlow's mind. At all events we regard the character in its reflected image, rather than in a direct gaze.

Although no novelist preaches less, Conrad's books are based on the axiom of the moral law. Ethically, his novels are sound. Perhaps the most impressive from the moral point of view is the long story, *Under Western Eyes,* where the student, who had everything to lose and nothing to gain by confession, suffered such intolerably acute agony of conscience (sharpened by love) that he could retain the truth not another moment; just as Raskolnikov, in *Crime and Punishment*, a book which this one in certain features resembles, had to give himself up to the police.

One reason why Conrad's characters with all the infinite detail we have of them do not seem so real as the persons in Jane Austen, is because the method of portraiture is not photographic. Each one of Jane Austen's men and women is an accurate reproduction. Conrad's people are made in the fusion of memory and thought. They are not given to the reader until the novelist has thought about them intensely. He sees them clearly but loves to speculate about them.

Two of his stories are quite different from the others. After all his studies of despair, it is interesting to read his charming, humorous, sympathetic and altogether delightful tale, *The Point of Honour*. It is a kind of allegory of the struggle between good and evil, with the triumph

of good.   For the other exception I can find in
my mind little favourable comment.   The story
Victory reads as though it were intended to gain
for its author a wider audience, as though he
had tried to write in a "popular" manner.   Despite many fine passages of description, it is
poor stuff, and its author should be ashamed of
Mr. Jones, who belongs to cheap melodrama.
It is to me inconceivable that Conrad should
deliberately lower his ideal, or hoist a white flag
to the hostile majority.   If that were true, *Victory* would be a defeat.   I regard it simply as
one of those lapses of which nearly all great
writers have shown themselves capable.

John Galsworthy is a notable figure in contemporary literature, having enjoyed something
like real fame for about ten years.   He is a
novelist and a dramatist of distinction; a maker
of respectable verse; above all, a satirist.   He
looks on the world with disapproval, and on
England with scorn; the latter attitude has of
course been modified by the war.   I used to wonder what all these writers who have used the
great middle-class of England as the butt of

their contempt and ridicule would do in the
event of a national crisis; for then the only
agency that could save England would be this
same despised middle-class. Well, they have
all become emotional—as emotional as pious dis-
senters—and solemnly "patriotic," except
Bernard Shaw. To him the British are as
ridiculous and contemptible in the hour of danger as they were in the days of safety.

His first important book was called *The Island
Pharisees,* which might stand as the title of his
complete works. Satire is here more prepon-
derant than art, and the novel falls by its weight.
The publication of this book seemed to cleanse
his bosom of much perilous stuff, for it was followed in two years by his masterpiece, *The Man
of Property,* one of the best English novels of
the twentieth century. There is a-plenty of satire, but the burlesques of the former book have
become real portraits. That family of brothers
is a triumph—"where do you get your wine, and
what do you pay for it?" Yet even in this fine
work occurs the obsession of Mr. Galsworthy, a
marriage without love, where the husband shows

intolerable cruelty in insisting on embracing his
wife, and hideous selfishness in objecting to her
gratifying her passions with another man.   The
husband is certainly an offensive person, and in
the Restoration Drama would have received appropriate frontal decorations; but the unpreju-
diced observer may enquire, If the lady did
not and could not love this man, why did she
marry him?   When women marry, some of them
anyhow are old enough to know better; and the
real test of character is not the making of an
unwise marriage, but the behaviour of a person
after the unwise marriage is made.   Mr. Galsworthy returns to this theme more than once,
and so overstates it in *The Fugitive* as to de-
prive the play of any hitting power.   For it is
not only the law of marriage he would have us
repeal, it is the law of causation.

Mr. Galsworthy insists that he is not a par-
tisan, but a chronicler; he is certainly acute,
thoroughly honest in purpose, and essentially
noble.   I like him best where he lives closest to
his creed, as in the account of the Forsyte family in *The Man of Property,* in the play *Strife,*

and in the most charming of all his novels, *The Patrician*. But he has an actively moral, as well as an artistic, conscience; his temperament is plainly radical, and his sympathies are always with those who are opposed to the present social organisation. The word Respectability makes him see red. No German has said worse things of England's hypocrisy than some of her own present-day novelists.

The much-praised *Country House* I found dull, and the only beneficial effect I obtained from its perusal was deep and refreshing sleep. *The Dark Flower* I found worse than dull; it is a blot in the fair 'scutcheon of its author. In his latest novel, *The Freelands*, a wise woman objects to visiting her sister-in-law because at her house she feels herself "all body"; in *The Dark Flower*, one has the same sensation. The characters are all body, and no soul. Every writer of noble mind—and Mr. Galsworthy surely belongs to that class—must desire not merely many readers, but the *best* readers, the most select, the most intelligent, the most critical. He wishes to have his works read primarily by those who are able to understand them. Now the penalty for emphasising instinct rather than thought, for analysing states of physical sensation rather than states of mind, is the lowering of one's clientèle. For example, a genius like Guy de Maupassant ought to be read only by the most intelligent men and women; whereas, thanks to his sex-obsession, the majority of his readers to-day all over the world are low-browed, morbid adolescents who find in him exactly what they are looking for. This will go on from generation to generation: instead of being read with mental delight, he will be read with a leer.

Despite all the foolish praise heaped upon Théophile Gautier, his most infamous novel holds its circulation through pornography; Mr. Booth Tarkington is quite right when he says that were it not for this element, it would not have twenty readers a year.

Out of the abundance of the heart the mouth speaketh. We expect base language from base minds. Therefore such a book as *The Dark Flower* coming from Mr. Galsworthy, is not only in itself distressing; it is a distressing surprise. He writes there as many men in the forties— dangerous years—secretly think; they are regretting the lost opportunities of their physical youth, regretting, not their sins, but old vetoes of conscience. Such a work as *The Dark Flower* has an unpleasantness that a writer of lower grade could not have produced; lilies that fester smell far worse than weeds.

The first half of *The Freelands* (1915) is wholly delightful; it has all the charm of *The Patrician,* with the added effect of even maturer art. In the burning of the rick the conflagration consumes not merely grass of the field, but all the natural beauty of the story; which straightway becomes tiresome and pedantic. The boy is a prig, and we can only hope that Nedda will remain as blind to his inherent dulness after marriage as she is before. The great redeeming feature of this novel is the character of Granny Freeland. She is as real as life itself; no one who pays any attention to her can help loving her. The unselfishness, resignation, tenderness, and gentleness that long years have taught her

contrast sharply with the egotistic dogmatic
assurance of her grandson. For, as Browning
says, the young man struts along as though he
owned the world; the old man walks the pave-
ment quietly, asking for nothing, merely hoping
that nobody will kill him. Her delightful little
remedies are ironically shown up by the author;
but after all, they are real remedies for real
(and curable) troubles.

A German who should read this book might
easily be pardoned for believing that the best
thing that could happen to Great Britain would
be its conquest by Germany.

J. M. Barrie, the greatest, most profound,
most original British dramatist of our time, is
so deservedly eminent in that field that we are
almost forgetting he belongs also in the history
of the English novel. To be sure, he has written only one masterpiece, *Sentimental Tommy,*
and he followed that with an inept sequel,
Tommy and Grizzel. In 1892 Stevenson wrote
to him, "I am proud to think you are a Scotch-
man. . . . I am a capable artist; but it begins
to look to me as if you were a man of genius."

A few months before his death, informed that he was the boy-model for *Sentimental Tommy*, he wrote, "My dear Barrie, I am a little in the dark about this new work of yours: what is to become of me afterwards? You say carefully —methought anxiously—that I was no longer me when I grew up? I cannot bear this suspense: what is it? It's no forgery? and *am I hangit?*"

The boy in *Sentimental Tommy* is just as truly the eternal boy as is Tom Sawyer; omit his love for the specific word, he has the charm, the imitativeness, the histrionic vein, the vanity, the laziness, the meanness, the colossal selfishness of all small boys. The Russians tell us not to blame the mirror if the face looks ugly. No honest man can read *Sentimental Tommy* without seeing himself reflected, minus the genius for composition. It is one of the most brilliant and most unpleasant works of our time; unpleasant because it does for every man what Hamlet did for his mother—it tells us what we really are. We cannot help being delighted with its humour—"don't say 'methinks' so often"

—but it has caused much melancholy and let us hope beneficial heart-searching.

The sequel, *Tommy and Grizzel,* was not needed. It is as though Mr. Barrie were afraid we should not see the moral, should not see our danger, should not see that the destination whither selfishness leads is tragic both for the protagonist and his associates; he therefore, throwing aside subtlety, roared a moral in our ears, pointing to the gibbet like any Hogarth. It was bad enough, in all conscience, to have Tess hanged, but to have Tommy hanged is like a very bad joke that leaves the whole company in an embarrassed silence.

> To die for faction is a common evil,
> But to be hanged for nonsense is the devil.

In the year 1904 Charlotte Brontë revisited the glimpses of the moon, wrote a strange novel called *The Divine Fire* and returned to the Elysian Fields. She signed the work by the then unfamiliar name of May Sinclair; and although the British audience for whom it was intended paid no attention to it, many thousands of Americans read it with such enthusiasm that echoes were aroused on the other side, and the English are now proud to claim what is theirs. In this particular literary conflagration, the divine fire was mingled with much smoke; but the flashes in the darkness were veritable flames, and May Sinclair is to-day the foremost living writer among English-speaking women. She has a hectic, feverish, high-tension manner that is not really unhealthy; it is more the overflowing of pent-up passion. For none of her books is made by the scraping together of what lies in the dusty corners of the mind; and no one of her books is made to order; they are more like escaping steam, that cannot be repressed another instant. They are the outcome, in other words, of fiercely held convictions. If she could not write, she would burst.

This white-hot intensity is just as characteristic of *The Helpmate, The Judgment of Eve, The Three Sisters, The Belfry,* as it is of *The Divine Fire*. *The Helpmate* and *The Judgment of Eve* represent exactly opposite points of view, for which, however, these two books afford excellent illustrations.   It is amusing to remember that when the former appeared in the *Atlantic Monthly,* there was a great fluttering in the Boston dovecotes; and if I remember rightly, some kind of editorial apology was demanded and given; it seemed that the first chapter was perused in the absence of the Head, and *that,* with the distinguished name of the author, was the warrant to advance at full speed.   But one steps on a firecracker in the very first chapter!

Miss Sinclair is a looker-on at the game of marriage, which gives her the vantage-ground for observing the mistakes of both players. *The Helpmate* castigates the woman, and *The Judgment of Eve* lashes the man.   The whip in each case descends on the guilty party, although women are sure to believe *The Helpmate* most needed, while men will own to the necessity of *The Judgment of Eve.*   We love and applaud all literary and oratorical castigation.   No man can read about the peevish importunity of the tuppenny husband over his outing suit, without feeling as David did when Nathan pushed the application home. I am sorry that *The Judgment of Eve* has not had a wider circulation. It is exactly the book which every reader will feel that his neighbours ought to read.

In *The Three Sisters,* Miss Sinclair approaches perihelion. This is the best book she has written, wrought with an art that has become thoroughly mature. The influence of the three Brontë sisters is more real than apparent; the spirit of the book shows the same unsatisfied thirst for life, the same frustration of passion, that one feels in *Jane Eyre* and in *Wuthering Heights*. Woman's inhumanity to woman is the basis of the plot; and although the scene is laid in a country parsonage, although the rector and his three daughters are all technically virtuous, the divine fire has become sulphurous; it is really the flame of hell. I know of no solution for the problem presented by the novelist except polygamy.

No *man* by any possiblity could ever have drawn that oldest sister; she is a "designing creature," presented with subtle art. This is a real novel, an important novel; it has a real story, startlingly real characters, has no thesis, and means nothing except as a significant representation of life.

The most steadily entertaining novel that Miss Sinclair has written is *The Belfry*. The last scenes are a concession to the dominating interest of the Great War, but they were necessary to bring out the character of the strange hero. This book again is filled with real people, and British "respectability" is treated, not with the scorn of Galsworthy, Bennett, and Wells, but with all a woman's patience for the stupidity and narrowness of humanity. Her "respectable" folk here are irritating at times, but they are charming too.

Miss Sinclair has made astonishing progress in literary art since the composition of *The Divine Fire;* there is no comparison at all between that book and *The Belfry*. No two of her books are alike; she is more than versatile: she has something of the range of humanity itself. What an extraordinary power of contrast is shown in the clergyman of *The Three Sisters* if you compare him with the Canter-

bury cleric in *The Belfry!* The two men, however, are no more unlike than the two books they
adorn. As Miss Sinclair grows older, her eyes
become more and more achromatic: in *The
Divine Fire,* she saw life through all kinds of
fantastic colours; now she sees the world as it
really is. And how infinitely more interesting
the actual world is than any of our illusions
about it!

Miss Mary Patricia Willcocks, of Devonshire,
is not nearly so well known as she deserves to
be. For many years a school-teacher, the
stream of her activity turned in 1905 to fiction,
and in 1907 she wrote a novel of great power
and charm, *The Wingless Victory.* The manuscript completely captured the heart of that
seasoned publisher, John Lane; nor do I think
any intelligent person could read this book
without feeling that the author belongs to literature. The most notable feature of her work is
its deep thoughtfulness, its active cerebration,
as different from the reflected culture of Mrs.
Ward as could well be imagined. She repeated
her success in 1908 with *A Man of Genius,* an-

other skilful diagnosis of human sickness.
Then, unfortunately, her later novels, *The Way
Up,* and *Wings of Desire,* while written with
real distinction, are too strongly flavoured with
the author's "opinions." The fact that she is
a feminist and naturally radical, ought not in
the least to have injured her literary work; for
she probably held the same convictions when
she wrote the *Wingless Victory.* No, she has
allowed her "views" to trespass in the pleasant
pastures of her art, where they seem at any rate
out of place.

But when I remember who she is, what she
has accomplished, and that she lives in Devon,
I have high hopes.

CHAPTER IX

Contemporary Novelists in Great Britain—Samuel Butler—Bernard Shaw—Eden Phillpotts—George Moore and the Experimental Novel—H. G. Wells—W. J. Locke—Alfred Ollivant—Mrs. W. K. Clifford—Mary Cholmondeley—W. B. Maxwell—Leonard Merrick—H. H. Bashford—A. S. M. Hutchinson—St. John Ervine.

I AM reminded of old Vigneron's remark about Meyerbeer; for Samuel Butler died without my noticing it; I didn't even know he was sick. Shortly after his cremated ashes had been scattered to the winds of heaven, a learned lady asked me if I knew anything about Samuel Butler. Although I have ceased to be shocked at anything the azure-footed say or do, I did feel a penumbra of chagrin, for I earn my bread by teaching English Literature. I proceeded to emit a few platitudes about *Hudibras,* when I was sharply interrupted, and informed that the subject for discussion was the *great* Samuel Butler, *the* Samuel Butler, "the greatest novel-est of the nineteenth century." This is a title that few writers of modern fiction have escaped, and I breathed easier. "Ignorance, Madam, pure ignorance,"—how often Johnson has helped us!

Now I am grateful to my fair tutor, for while the name of the Erewhon philosopher must eventually have penetrated even into academic circles, I might have remained a few months longer in the outer darkness, and thus have postponed my acquaintance with *The Way of All Flesh*. Butler spent a good many years writing this extraordinary book, and finished it a good many years ago, but in 1902, on his deathbed, gave for the first time, permission to have it printed, characteristically reversing the conventional deathbed repentance and confession. He, who had abandoned all faith except in his own infallibility, ardently believed in his posthumous fame, which has become a reality. Its slow growth seems to indicate permanence.

It is a curious fact that the two Samuel Butlers—the seventeenth century poet and the nineteenth century novelist—should have held pre-

cisely the same attitude toward religious prig-
gery. Neither could endure the organised
and dominant church-going-christianity of his
epoch. What the Burlesquer said of the Puritans neatly expresses the contempt felt by his
namesake.

> A sect whose chief devotion lies
> In odd, perverse antipathies,
> In falling out with that or this
> And finding somewhat still amiss;
> More peevish, cross, and splenetic
> Than dog distract or monkey sick:
> That with more care keep holyday
> The wrong, than others the right way;
> Compound for sins they are inclined to
> By damning those they have no mind to.

And the late W. E. Henley's summary of the
first Samuel Butler fits the second almost without the change of a word. I give it verbatim.
"He had an abundance of wit of the best and
truest sort; he was an indefatigable observer;
he knew opinions well, and books even better;
he had considered life acutely and severely; as
a rhythmist he proceeded from none and has had
no successor; his vocabulary is of its kind in-

comparable; his work is a very hoard of sentences and saws, of vigorous locutions and picturesque colloquialisms, of strong sound sense and robust English.''

Bernard Shaw, taking his eye off Brieux for a moment, informed us that he learned more from Butler than from any other writer; a statement easier to believe than some of his affirmations. Unfortunately the disciple is so much above his lord in popular estimation, that we have all been withholding honour where honour is due. After one has read Butler, one sees where many of Shaw's perversities and ironies came from. The foundation of Butler's style is the paradox; moral dynamics are reversed; the unpardonable sin is conventionality. His masterpiece answers no questions; solves no problems; chases away no perplexities. Every reader becomes an interrogation point. Butler rubs our thoughts the wrong way. As axiom after axiom is ruthlessly attacked, we pick over our minds for some missile to throw at him. It is a good thing for every man and woman whose brain happens to be in activity to read this amazingly clever, original, brilliant, diabolical novel. And for those whose brains are in captivity it may smash some fetters. Every one who understands what he reads will take an inventory of his own religious and moral stock.

Butler delighted in the rôle of Advocatus Diaboli: in his *Note-Books* he has the following apology for the Devil: "It must be remembered that we have heard only one side of the case. God has written all the books." Well, He certainly did not write this one; He permitted the Devil to have his hour. The worst misfortune that can happen to any person, says Butler, is to lose his money; the second is to lose his health; and the loss of reputation is a bad third. He seems to have regarded the death of his father as the most fortunate event in his own life; for it made him financially independent. He never quite forgave the old man for hanging on till he was eighty years old. He ridiculed the Bishop of Carlisle for saying that we long to meet our parents in the next world. "Speaking for myself, I have no wish to see my father

again, and I think it likely that the Bishop of
Carlisle would not be more eager to see his than
I mine." Melchisedec "was a really happy
man. He was without father, without mother,
and without descent. He was an incarnate
bachelor. He was a born orphan."

One reason why *The Way of All Flesh* is becoming every year more widely known, is because it happens to be exactly in the literary
form most fashionable in fiction at this moment.
It is a "life" novel—it is a biography, which of
course means that it is very largely an autobiography. Three generations of the hero's
family are portrayed with much detail; the plot
of the story is simply chronological; the only
agreeable woman in the book was a personal
friend of the author. Not only are hundreds
of facts in the novelist's own life minutely recorded, it is a spiritual autobiography as well.
It was his habit—also true of Arnold Bennett—
to carry a notebook in his pocket; whenever a
thought or fancy occurred to him, immediately
to write it down. An immense number of these
fatherless ideas are now inwoven in this novel.

The result is that the reader literally finds
something interesting and often something valuable on every page. The style is so closely
packed with thought that it produces constant
intellectual delight. This is well; for I can recall no delight of any other kind.

Just as Samuel Butler poured out in *Hudibras*
the accumulated bottled venom and hatred of
many years, so our novelist has released all the
repugnance, the rebellion, the impotent rage of
childhood. He had an excellent memory, and
seems to have forgiven nothing and forgotten
nothing that happened to him in the dependent
years of his life. It is an awkward thing to
play with souls, and Butler represents the souls
of boys treated by their parents and by their
school-teachers with astonishing stupidity and
blundering brutality. It is a wonderful treatise
on the art of how *not* to bring up children; and
I should think that every mother, father, and
teacher would feel some sense of shame and
some sense of fear. For a good many years
children are in the power of their elders, who
so greatly excel them in both physical strength

and in cunning; but every child, no matter how dutifully he may kiss the rod, becomes in after years the Judge of his parents and of his teachers. Butler's sympathy with children, whose little bodies and little minds are often in absolute bondage to parents both dull and cruel, is a salient quality in his work. One is appalled when one remembers how often the sensitive soul of a little boy is tortured at home, simply by coarse handling. This championship of children places Butler with Dickens, though I suppose such a remark would have been regarded by Butler as an insult.

I think that the terrific attack on "professing Christians" made in this novel will be of real service to Christianity. Just as men of strong political opinions have largely abandoned the old habit of reading the party paper, and now give their fiercest opponents a hearing, so I think good Christian people will derive much benefit from an attentive perusal of this work. The religion that Butler attacks is the religion of the Scribes and Pharisees, and unless our religion exceeds that, none of us is going to enter the Kingdom of Heaven. The Church needs clever, active antagonists to keep her up to the mark; the principle of Good is toughened by constant contact with the principle of Evil; every minister ought to have in his audience a number of brilliant, determined opponents, who have made up their minds they will believe nothing he says; I have no doubt that God needs the Devil.

Thus, although I firmly believe this is a diabolical novel, I think it will prove to be of service to Christianity. I know it has done me good. I cannot forget Butler's remark about all those church-goers who would be equally shocked if any one doubted Christianity or if any one practised it.

Butler's attitude toward everything except Händel and himself was ironical; he delighted in ridiculing any generally accepted tenet in politics, science, art, and religion. This was often done behind a mask of grave, candid enquiry, in the manner of Swift. Even his personal appearance was ironical, for although he could truthfully have said "I have fought the good faith,'' he looked like a devout, and rather ignorant evangelical parson.[1]

Butler's most famous disciple, Mr. Shaw, would be a novelist of high reputation were it not for the fact that, like Mr. Barrie, he has achieved greater renown in another field. Yet *Cashel Byron's Profession* is just as good a novel in 1916 as it was in the eighties, when it was written; and we all know the enthusiasm it awakened in Stevenson, who read it when its author's name had no significance. In sheer literary excellence Shaw's later and more famous works do not surpass this book; and it possesses one quality absent in all the plays, both pleasant and unpleasant; it has an irresistible charm. Like many pacifists, Shaw is not greatly shocked at prize-fighting; the way of the world, of course, is to regard professional boxing as brutal, and war as noble and sublime, even ''holy.''

Although, with the exception of Thomas

[1] The preceding remarks on Butler are taken by kind permission of E. P. Dutton and Company, from my Introduction to their American edition of *The Way of All Flesh*, published in 1916.

Hardy, there is no titanic figure among British novelists of the present moment, the number of professional novelists of high standing is nothing less than remarkable. I wonder at the diffusion of talent. I think I could name twenty-five English writers of the twentieth century whose novels have dignity and distinction, who are reliable—who can be depended on to produce something worth reading. A large company of literary experts have mastered the art of fiction, and while they do not always give us a good story, or construct a good plot, the proportion of success in their rapid production is high, and even the less notable part of their work is free from anything shoddy. An epitome of the general level of excellence, a fine representative of the whole school, is seen in Eden Phillpotts, of Devonshire. Without a single flash of genius, and with a pseudo-scientific creed that is irritating, Mr. Phillpotts writes three or four novels a year, every one of which has value—and, what is particularly surprising, every one seems deeply thought out, carefully wrought, full of meat. It ought to

take him three years to write any one of these
books, instead of three months, which is all the
time he can apparently spare.   Like his master,
Thomas Hardy, he is a good deal of a pagan,
though not altogether a pessimist; and like his
master, he has a deep, genuine vein of humour,
which brightens his darkest tragedies, and con-
stitutes the chief element in his most charming
story, *Widecombe Fair.*   Just as in some of
his novels, a tor, a river, or a moor is one of
the chief characters, in this book the leading
actor is the village.   There is no hero or heroine; we follow the fortunes of a group, and the
author's studies of Dartmoor end on a note of
pure comedy.   One should read his preface to
Widecombe Fair, and follow his advice.   He
salutes the finished work of twenty years, answers his critics, and insists on his undoubted
right to be judged by all the Dartmoor books
taken together, rather than by any one.   In the
work of twenty years he has tried to express his
creed of affirmation in life, which he thinks
chokes pessimism; if pessimism be mere acqui-
escence, it could indeed not breathe on those

heights. But the affirmation itself in these novels means tragedy, and a final tragic answer to life is not entirely removed from pessimism.

Mr. Phillpotts is at his best when he stays in his corner, both in time and space; his least successful books are *The Lovers*—a historical romance, which seems to be directly aimed at an American audience, and *The Joy of Youth,* which skips blithely to Italy. Both these stories were published in 1913. His solid qualities as a novelist shine most conspicuously in *The Secret Woman* (1905), *The Portreeve* (1906), *The Three Brothers* and *The Haven* (both 1909), and *The Thief of Virtue* (1910). I think *The Three Brothers* is his best novel, and the one that shows most brilliantly his powers of characterisation.

Although he bade farewell to Dartmoor in 1913, he did not travel very far from his beloved country in *Brunel's Tower* (1915), a novel full of vitality. The protagonist is a pottery, whose centripetal power draws in all the characters, yes, and the reader, too; for we become as interested in the place as any of the

workmen.   The specific problem of the story is
the struggle between evil antecedents and dog-
like affection to a patron; this struggle takes
place in the soul of an altogether charming boy.
The conflict is in doubt until almost the last
page, when the victory is won at the highest
possible price.

Like Rudyard Kipling, Mr. Phillpotts was
born in India and educated in Devon.   Perhaps
his ardent love for the mists of the moors has
been strengthened by the intolerable sunshine
of the land of his birth.

No man takes his art more seriously than he;
no man believes more profoundly in the dignity
of the novel.   When we remember that both
Jane Austen and Henry James assumed a defensive attitude, the advance of the novel in
the twentieth century is conspicuously shown by
what Mr. Phillpotts wrote for the New York
Times, 22 August, 1915: "The art of the novel
embraces every sort of mental interest. . . .
Among those who regard novel writing as man's
work, and the noblest of arts—among those of
fine natural endowment who approach it with

sincerity and their full strength—shall be found the best writers of the English language at present living. It is not too much to say that contemporaries have written some of the best novels in our tongue, but to state this is not to disparage the pioneer masters. Fielding and Richardson had a different field to play upon, and the art has developed so enormously, the models from other nations have worked such wonders, that the novel as written in England and America now challenges the finest intellects and greatest artists of the time. The very fire of life glows in this art, and its possibilities are beyond all prediction, for fiction is the greatest education force in the modern world.''

The Zola type of experimental novel has never been popular in England, as it has in France, Germany, Italy, Sweden, and Russia; it is bunkered by the English conscience. Although France and England are separated by only twenty miles of salt-water, their traditional attitudes toward art are as different as though the two countries were on separate planets. Just why such intimate neighbours should show so tremendous a parallax in their view of art may be left to some one else to explain; the fact is clear enough, when we remember that Guy de Maupassant read all his manuscripts to his mother, and that Alphonse Daudet thought *Sapho* a good book for his son. The foremost living representative of the experimental novel in England is George Moore, who is not English at all, but an Irishman with a French education, like Oscar Wilde. George Moore is a true disciple of Zola; he takes realistic art very seriously, and solemnly announces that his chief recreation is religion. Wordsworth's *Prelude* seems scanty, when we remember that George Moore has written the history of his own life in five volumes; and although the latest one is called *Vale,* it may be so only in a Pattian sense. Not one of these autobiographies is as truthful as *Esther Waters* or *Evelyn Innes;* conversations with distinguished people are reported at great length and with much detail, conversations that may never have occurred. And while Mr. Moore insists in telling us all about his amours, the facts in every case may be reasonably doubted. All of these pages of alleged biographical sensuality are really senile—it is like a weak old man licking his lips.

Some one has said that George Moore has never recovered from his surprise at having written a really good book—*Esther Waters,* which appeared in the memorable year of 1894. Previously, he had produced a number of experimental novels, that were perhaps more experiments than novels. I refer to *A Modern Lover* (1883), *A Mummer's Wife* (1884), *Spring Days* (1888), *Mike Fletcher* (1889). These books all show a certain artistic sincerity, a strenuous simplicity of style, without any real power of characterisation; they would not have attracted any attention at all, were it not for their lubricity. No one seemed to admire the author, or to take him seriously. All he had acquired was notoriety, "the bastard sister of reputation"; and his notoriety was of a decidedly unsavoury kind. Then, with the appearance of *Esther Waters,* he conquered his public, both in England and America. By the irony of fate, the book was widely advertised as a moral tract; many thousand copies of a cheap edition were circulated with a horrible cover design; with a loud label to the effect that this novel was the "Uncle Tom's Cabin of the White Slaves." Knowing George Moore's ideas as we do, this perversity of advertising puffery had a humour all its own. One might more easily imagine the late Thomas Huxley as a Gospel evangelist.

The extraordinary merit of *Esther Waters* was immediately recognised by good judges. Like Pamela, Esther is a housemaid, who passes through various adventures, retaining the interest, the sympathy, and the admiration of the reader. It is a masterpiece in the experimental school; there are no comments, no doctrines, no teachings; and there is nothing superfluous. I marvel at the economy of design, at the economy of language; it seems as if there were not a superfluous word in the book. Without once raising his voice, Mr. Moore holds our closest attention from first page to last. For one cannot read this work of fiction without believing that everything in it is the living truth. If one wishes to know the difference between realistic art and sensational daubing, one has merely to read the account of Derby Day in *Esther Waters* and then compare it with the rhetorical version in *The Christian,* by Hall Caine. Although I have never seen the Derby, I experienced all the pleasures of recognition in George Moore's account of it.

Even if not intended by the author, *Esther Waters* has a nobly ethical tone; the tone of sincerity and truth. No one can read it without admiration for its author's skill, or without feeling a moral stimulation.

This extraordinary novel was a turning-point in the author's career. While he has not written anything since of quite equal value, the difference between the novels that came after *Esther Waters* and those that preceded it, is the difference between an intellectually robust man and a morbid boy. The three novels, *Evelyn Innes* (1898), the sequel *Sister Teresa* (1901), and *The Lake* (1905), are all notable works of art; all emphatically worth reading and re-reading. I can see how some critics might regard *The Lake* as his best work; it has a subdued, a restrained power, that takes a permanent place in the memory. The discussions of music in *Evelyn Innes* are immensely interesting to the amateur; and inasmuch as Evelyn was a prima donna, I felt high curiosity in asking the late Madame Nordica what she thought of the book. She had nothing but contempt for it, saying the remarks on music were of no value whatever, and that they revealed appalling ignorance. Then I asked a distinguished opera composer; he replied that the musical knowledge displayed was very remarkable, and that the discussions of music were valuable and interesting.

For my part, having no right to an opinion on the merits of this question, the wonderful *Vorspiel* to *Lohengrin* has taken on a new significance for me after reading the conversation about it between Evelyn and the nun.

George Moore's short stories are like a grey day in Ireland. One of those in *Celibates* was written apparently under the influence of Russian naturalism.

Twenty years ago, while doing some reviewing for a New York journal, I received a package of new novels. The title of one of them caught my fancy, though I had never heard of the author. It was *The Wheels of Chance,* by H. G. Wells. He had been a maker of books less than a twelvemonth, though prophetically prolific, having published four separate volumes the first year of his career, 1895. It may be a damaging admission, but while I have a high respect for the ability of Mr. Wells, I have never enjoyed reading any one of his novels so much as I enjoyed *The Wheels of Chance.* One may roar with laughter at *Bealby* (1915), but there is no more delicacy in its humour than in a farce-film; whereas *The Wheels of Chance,* describing the bicycle adventures of Mr. Hoopdriver, the dry-goods clerk, has something of the combined mirth, pathos, and tenderness of Don Quixote. There is not a hint in this little book of Wells the Socialist, Wells the Reformer, Wells the Futurist, Wells· the Philosopher— there is only Wells the artist, whom I admire more than I do the sociological preacher.

I am quite willing to admit that it is the more pretentious Wells who has become the world-figure, for a world-figure he undoubtedly is. Before the Great War, his books were in the window of every important book-shop in Germany, where he was studied rather than read. French and Russian translations poured from the press year after year. And yet I am not at all sure that he has made any real contribution to modern thought, whereas he has made a distinct contribution to modern literary art. He writes books faster than any one can read them; faster than any one publisher can produce them, as may be seen by a reference to his bibliography. Yet as a rule his work is neither shallow nor trivial.

In one respect he has never fulfilled the promise of *The Wheels of Chance*. There was a touch of spirituality in that playful comedy, a flash that has since been altogether obscured by the cloudy sky of materialism. It seems unfortunate that when Mr. Wells has so many gifts, so much talent, he has not the little more, and how much it is! He is a man of prose, downright, hard-headed, matter-of-fact. One could hardly expect him to write like Nathaniel Hawthorne, but it is a pity that he should be as far removed from Hawthorne as a railway timetable. How is it possible for a man to have so much humour and be so limited? Yet that kind comes only by prayer and fasting, words that have no meaning for Mr. Wells.

Many of his stories are like a dusty road, as Scott's are like a thick forest. We reach certain elevations and see ahead of us nothing but the long brown way, in the pitiless glare of the sun. That was my feeling all through *Ann Veronica.* I liked *Marriage* much better, though the wilderness-cure was a large order. I liked *The Wife of Sir Isaac Harman* better yet, for it contains an admirable commingling of the two authors living in the brain of Mr. Wells, the author of *The Wheels of Chance, Kipps* and *Bealby*—and the man who wrote *Ann Veronica* and *Marriage.* For he is a dual personality, as his friend Arnold Bennett is—what a difference between the serious and the trivial Bennett!

The wife of Sir Isaac is a lovely woman, full

of charm. She married the impossible Isaac
because she could not be sufficiently disobliging
to cause him the annoyance or even the incon-
venience of a refusal. This marriage turned
out altogether bad, worse than her soft heart's
imaginings. Death released her; in the first
sweets of freedom appears the "damned literary man," who, in contrast to Sir Isaac, seemed
at first to bear healing in his wings. But
closer inspection reveals this secretary-bird to
be a goose, with the futile gabble and peevish
disposition of the goose. The comedy of the
last scene is wholly delightful. The shy, gentle
woman, wearing the colour of freedom—black
—shyly, gently, but decisively refuses him in
the garden. Like a spoiled child who has been
refused a toy, like the hero of a French novel
who has been deprived of his mistress, the man
of letters rushes away down the rainy garden
path, crying, weeping, sobbing, roaring out his
woe to the circumambient air. This is too much
for the soft-hearted Mrs. Harman; she cannot
bear to behold such suffering. Faint, yet pur-
suing, she reaches the breathless hero, and we

leave her as she enters slavery a second time. Perhaps, had she been more resolute, more wise—perhaps we should not love her so much.

If the English have no sense of humour, their writers must furnish the exceptions that prove the rule. I can think of no living English novelist of distinction who is not a humourist, and of only one among the dead—Samuel Richardson. Hardy, De Morgan, Bennett, Wells, Phillpotts, Ollivant, Chesterton, Hutchinson, Lucas, Hawkins, Beerbohm, Locke, Merrick, Elinor Mordaunt—they are all humourists, each in his own degree and with his own special flavour. Nor would it be possible to deny the title altogether to John Galsworthy.

Among contemporary men of letters, one of the best-beloved is William John Locke, who has made large additions to the gaiety of nations, and who is trying to justify two-thirds of his name by a considerable amount of original and sound philosophy. This man took the steep and thorny road to the heaven of literary fame, by graduating mathematical tripos at St. John's College, Cambridge. There is no doubt that a large proportion of successful novelists and dramatists have exhibited high talent in the study of mathematics. The constructive ability, the skill in original problems, very often bears fruit later in original literary work. The most conspicuous example at present is Thomas Hardy, whose professional training as an architect appears in every one of his novels, giving them a solidity and beauty of construction entirely beyond the range of all his living contemporaries. There cannot be the slightest doubt that Mr. Locke's honours in mathematics and his successful professional work as an architect have been of immense service in his brilliant career as a novelist.

Mr. Locke has exactly what Mr. Wells has not—the power to make his readers love him. We all admire the enormous industry and the mental vigour of H. G. Wells—we admire these qualities without feeling any affection for the author; he is a high-power machine-gun in modern fiction, making Hawthorne look like a muzzle-loading musket. But we feel no more love for him than for a load of bricks. In all the novels of W. J. Locke there is pervading warmth of heart. In *Septimus* (1909), his most humorous book, he has, by sheer capacity for affection, made two heroes out of the most unpromising material. Sypher is a vulgar, blatant patent-medicine advertiser; he bears the same relation to a gentleman that a steam calliope bears to a violin. Septimus is a harmless nincompoop, about as aggressive as a wounded rabbit. Yet, by "God's passionless reformers, influences," both these men are transformed into true heroes, and when we take leave of them, we stand uncovered.

This novel *Septimus* is one of the funniest books of the twentieth century. It is the only novel of this century that I have been unable to read to myself in the presence of strangers. As a rule, no matter how comic the situations may be in the book you hold in your hand, if it be a public place, your countenance betrays nothing of the roaring mirth in your brain; you are enjoying every word with no demonstrations. I attempted to read *Septimus* on the train, and came near to being ejected. The sud-

den surprises of the humour were so great that
I vented prodigious cachinnations, which
shocked me as much as they did the passengers.
I can see those passengers, now, turning around,
craning their necks, looking with raised eye-
brows at their insane associate. The hours
Septimus selected for his meals, his method of
servant annunciation, his scheme for avoiding
railway accidents—no one has any right to be
so funny!

There is a remarkable progression in Mr.
Locke's most famous novels—a distinct progression from paganism to Christianity. Although he had published a number of books in
the nineteenth century, he attracted not much
attention until 1905, when *The Morals of Mar-
cus Ordeyne* appeared. Personally I cared little for this story—the return of Eve is *vieux
jeu,* although the author has tried it once more
in *Jaffery* (1915). But it was unmistakably
the work of a literary expert, almost dazzlingly
brilliant. It was also pagan, no hint of a Christian point of view. It was followed the next
year by what many regard as his masterpiece,

The Beloved Vagabond—delightful, charming, witty—with no indication of a moral basis, the ethics being as footloose as the hero. Three years passed, and in *Septimus* the central Christian idea of sacrifice was the foundation of the plot. Then came *Simon the Jester,* a story analogous to Browning's *Light Woman,* which, to be sure, Mr. Hornung had already taken in *No Hero.* This novel is illumined with deep religious feeling, and as if to leave no doubt on the subject, Mr. Locke gave us later his sincere and beautiful *Three Wise Men.*

In *The Glory of Clementina Wing* (1911) we have again Mr. Locke the ethical philosopher. His later books are essays of a rather different nature, and are not nearly so successful; the *Fortunate Youth* is a rather pointless extravaganza, and while *Jaffery* is an immense improvement, it cannot compare in beauty and charm with *The Beloved Vagabond* or *Septimus.*

Mr. Alfred Ollivant in 1898 produced the best dog story ever written—*Bob, Son of Battle,* a story distinctly superior to *Rab,* to *The Bar Sinister,* and to *The Call of the Wild.* It has already become a classic, although it has a thousand readers in America to a dozen in England. There is not a town of any size in the United States that does not contain ardent lovers of this powerful and beautiful novel; yet it is very rare that one meets an Englishman who has even heard of it. I have never met one, though I have asked the question many times; and it was refreshing when I enquired of the Scot, J. M. Barrie, if he knew *Owd Bob,* to hear him say, "Well, rather!"

Since the appearance of *Romola,* moral decay has been a favourite study of English novelists; and although we know what Ruskin thought of the *Decline and Fall,* we do not care. For we know well enough the ethical value of the study of decadence, whether the patient be a nation or an individual. Browning, with all his hearty faith, did not hesitate to study the decay of love; and one of the most brilliant presentations of this common phenomenon appears in an extremely clever work of fiction published in 1891 by Mrs. W. K. Clifford, *Love Letters of a Worldly Woman;* which has for its text, a citation from *One Word More*—"Wherefore? Heaven's gift takes earth's abatement." This book follows Richardson's example in everything but length, being cast in the form of letters. There is a delicate psychological analysis here that one cannot read without mental pleasure. Mrs. Clifford has produced many works since then, and I hope she will write many more. But she has never done anything quite equal in artistic precision to that tiny, early masterpiece.

Miss Cholmondeley, with her sombre talent, ought to write something in this vein better than she has thus far succeeded in accomplishing. While reading *Red Pottage* and especially *Prisoners*, I am conscious of a tremendous latent power that does not reach the printed page. Is her difficulty merely one of articulation?

Two brilliant studies of moral decay in the individual may be seen in two recent novels: I refer to *In Cotton Wool* (1912) by W. B. Maxwell, and to *Tributaries* (1914) (American title, *The House of Deceit*), by an English author who wishes to remain anonymous. *In*

Cotton Wool has a sloping descent that makes the first chapter and the last as different as the Lilliputians and the Yahoos; its purpose is purely ethical, its art absolutely sincere. The line of least resistance leads to hell. In *Tributaries,* we have another melancholy but ethically valuable picture of slow and subtle moral deterioration. The hero's course is not straight down, but in spirals; he rises a little after each relapse, only to sink deeper on the next slide, and eventually to become an incurable case—a lost soul.

The level of the work of Leonard Merrick is high, but it would have been better for his fame had he written ten worthless books and one masterpiece. He is a novelist of real distinction, incapable of producing sensational, cheap, superficial, or stodgy books. The oft-quoted bull exactly fits his work: although he seldom rises above his average, he never falls below it. Any one of his novels may be safely recommended to beguile the tedium of a railway journey; railway travel is generally as disagreeable as an operation, and one should always take an anæsthetic. With a good novel, the patient reaches his destination unaware of the jolts and stops that punctuated progress.

There is a shocking sincerity in the work of H. H. Bashford that ought to carry him far on the road toward permanent fame. In *The Pilgrims' March,* we have scenes that find their only counterpart in *Fanny's First Play.* In a more powerful, and much more disagreeable story, *Pity the Poor Blind,* we have a picture of life in an English country house that I ardently hope is untrue. The study of the self-deceived clergyman converted by a perfectly rudimentary and perfectly healthy female, is not easy to forget. Perhaps the most original character in the story is the little sister. In the course of my adventures in fiction, I have met many limbs of Satan, in the perfect disguise of innocent girlhood. Yet never anything to compare with this creature. She is not an *enfant terrible;* she is a child of hell.

Delightful it is to turn from the sulphurous laughter of Mr. Bashford to the wholesome outdoor heartiness of Mr. A. S. M. Hutchinson. In *The Happy Warrior* (1912), he created the most irresistibly winsome boy that I have ever met, in or out of books—"Did you say Getap?" Like Mercutio, he was too good to last—the author had to kill him. Yet the death of Mercutio is a vital factor in the plot of Shakespeare's tragedy, whereas there was no necessity for the death of our young warrior. In *A Clean Heart* (1914), we have the very extremes of emotion. No one whose nerves are askew should read the first third of the book; it is a terrible picture of mental obsession becoming madness. I thought I was going to lose my mind. The scene changes from the horror of insanity to such outrageous mirth, horse-play, buffoonery, that one forgets approaching madness and holds one's sides in a veritable agony of laughter. The egoist learns Christianity first from a roaring drunkard and then from an ignorant girl; learns the truth only by the sacrifice of two persons perhaps more valuable than he. This is a deeply religious book; illustrat-

ing with striking power the Scriptural text that
supplies the title. Mr. Hutchinson bids fair to
be a vital force in modern fiction.

Mr. St. John Ervine, the Irish dramatist,
published in 1914 a sombre and depressing
novel called *Mrs. Martin's Man*—not by any
means a wholly successful book, but truly
original, quite out of the ordinary and conventional rut. His next story, *Alice and a Family,*
is one of the most charming, enliveningly humorous character-sketches of our time. The
dialogue has a steady brilliance that is astonishing; no lapses from beginning to end. It is
a story of the London slums exactly as *The
Rosie World* is a story of the New York slums.
And the resemblance is carried much further,
for in each instance it is a little girl who pulls
the strings. If each family in the world had
either a Rosie or an Alice, the millennium would
materialise.

CHAPTER X

TWENTIETH CENTURY AMERICAN NOVELISTS

The leading contemporary Americans—Losses by death and depreciation—James Lane Allen—Charles Stewart—H. K. Viele—Henry Harland—Owen Wister—Winston Churchill—Art and politics—Booth Tarkington—The Indiana School—Jack London—Robert Herrick—H. S. Harrison—Gertrude Atherton—Mary Wilkins—Edith Wharton—Dorothy Canfield—Anne Sedgwick.

SOME Americans of promise have been defeated by death; others have been beaten by their own past. A conspicuous example of the first class is Frank Norris; of the second, James Lane Allen. No matter what one's ambition may be —poetry, engineering, social prestige, dancing, tennis—there are plenty of active and merciless competitors; but the most active and the most merciless is one's own self. The history of athletics is the tragedy of the athlete trying to keep up with himself, and invariably being beaten. The biography of nearly every professional baseball player is the melancholy circle—

from oblivion to the minor league to the major
league to the minor league to oblivion. He
completes this orbit in about the time it takes
Jupiter to go once around the sun. But the
path of the literary man ought to be as the shining light, that shineth more and more unto the
perfect day. Seldom is this the case. Blackmore wrote *Lorna Doone,* and spent thirty
strenuous years in a losing race with himself.
Kipling, in the prime of life, cannot recapture
the first, fine, careless rapture—and how earnestly he tries; with what bulldog determination!
To produce one work of genius is perhaps
enough for a lifetime; and yet there must be the
very passion of failure in the realisation that
one cannot equal one's past mental achieve-
ments. Many authors know in their own hearts
what Swift meant when, turning over the pages
of *A Tale of a Tub,* he cried out, "Good God,
what a genius I had when I wrote that book!"

When *The Choir Invisible* appeared in 1897
it received both in England and in America the
acclaim it richly deserved. Since that time Mr.
Allen has been led astray from the fields of art

by some kind of portentous philosophy. Even
a *good* creed will often wreck an artist; but
when the light that is in him is darkness, how
great is that darkness! To see how far from
truth and nature a philosophical scheme will
drag a really intelligent writer, one has only to
read *The Bride of the Mistletoe* (1909). This
story is not meant to be a "gramercy" book;
it is not intended to be a high-flown historical
romance. No, it describes a modern college
professor's conversations with his wife; and
they have been married a goodly number of
years. Now when a man and a woman have
been married ten years, they know each other
rather well; whatever the mask worn in public,
however successful the man may be in the
rhetorical deceit of strangers, at home there is
a person on whom this kind of thing won't work.
Yet this is the way Mr. Allen's college professor
talks to his own wife; talks to her when they
are alone, without a gallery:

"Josephine, sometimes while looking out of
the study window a spring morning, I have
watched you strolling among the flowers of the

lawn. I have seen you linger near a honey-
suckle in full bloom and question the blossoms
in your questioning way—you who are always
wishing to probe to the heart of things, to drain
out of them the red drop of their significance.
But, grey-eyed querist of actuality, those fragrant trumpets could blow to your ear no message about their origin.''

Now what would happen to a man in the
twentieth century who should address his wife
(when no one else was around) as ''grey-eyed
querist of actuality''? She would either burst
into irrepressible laughter or, after an anxious scrutiny, she would take his tempera-
ture.

If this book were the work of some gushing
girl—but it isn't; it was written by a trained
novelist of distinction, a man who has honestly
earned fame by a notable story. Yet to those
who are wondering what is the matter with Mr.
Allen, *The Bride of the Mistletoe* is instructive
and explanatory. To me such rhodomontade in
a novel is as unpleasant as sanctimonious cant,
or the bunkum we hear from those ''friends of

the workingman,'' the candidates for political office.

The American novelist most worthy to fill the particular vacancy caused by the death of Mark Twain is Charles D. Stewart. His literary production is varied, both in subject-matter and in excellence; and he has written two novels that are genuine studies of American life, informed with rich humour—*The Fugitive Blacksmith* (1905) and *Partners of Providence* (1907). In the former, the story of the man left alone with the sheep and driven mad by the stars is art of high sincerity. In the latter, there are two leading characters, the Mississippi and the Missouri. These mighty rivers become mighty personalities. This is the book that in vividness of description, accurate reporting, lively imagination, and roaring mirth infallibly reminds the reader of Mark Twain.

The death of Herman Knickerbocker Viele in 1908 robbed American literature of a brilliant novelist. His *Last of the Knickerbockers* contains pictures of a New York boarding-house worthy of Balzac; it is a novel combining realism, wit and tenderness with a certain delicacy of touch rare on this side of the ocean. His other story, *The Inn of the Silver Moon* (1900), has a grace, humour, and charm worthy of the French scene where it is laid. It seems strange that work of such distinction did not attract more general attention; but Mr. Viele would surely have received adequate recognition if he had lived longer.

The late Henry Harland made an artistic mistake in turning from tragedy to comedy, from the slums of New York to the beauty of the Italian lakes. Financially it was a profitable speculation; for one reader of *As It Was Written* there were a hundred of *The Cardinal's Snuff Box*. His later manner was as agreeable as rich food and sparkling wine; his books were eagerly devoured and speedily forgotten. But some of us can still remember the thrill in reading that story of double personality where the lover stabbed his betrothed in the night, and was overwhelmed with horror and amazement to find her body in the morning. "Sydney Luska" was a more impressive writer than

Henry Harland—and it was a pity that he joined the marshmallow school.

Owen Wister, in *The Virginian,* succeeded in accomplishing a difficult task. He produced a "best seller" that continues to sell. This admirable novel was the American literary sensation of the year 1902, and unlike most sensations, has not been forgotten. Had the work contained more unity, had the different episodes been more skilfully welded, we might have seen a classic. As it is we have one of the best works of American fiction of the twentieth century, incomparably better than anything else its author has achieved, though his other books—especially *Philosophy Four*—are not without distinction.

Mr. Winston Churchill produced *Richard Carvel* in 1899, and his steady production of "C" novels that have followed at regular intervals has been one continuous stream of popular success. He is far more a *representative* of modern American literature than he is a leader of it; for he is surely as remarkable for his limitations as for his virtues. He has learned how to write novels by writing them; he has become a finished expert. The crudities of his earlier work have been ironed out; he reports the salient features of American social, political and religious life. His characters are chosen, not created; they are chosen to represent the ideas that Mr. Churchill wishes to convey to his readers. An honest and high-minded man, with the unmistakable temperament of a reformer, Mr. Churchill seems to feel the responsibility of his popularity. As he sits down at his desk to begin a new novel, he has the comforting and also terrifying assurance that five hundred thousand people will read and discuss the sentences he writes in solitude. He must do something to improve the world. Thus his novels are becoming more and more didactic. His finest work is seen in *Coniston* (1906), and even there he is more "progressive" than artistic. In the *Inside of the Cup* (1913) he devoutly, reverently, and energetically attacked the modern church; in *A Far Country* (1915), which comes dangerously near the limbo of tedium, he attacked the modern conditions of commercial life. If he does not change his tactics he may share the fate of Mrs. Humphry Ward, whose so-called novels have sunk under an accumulation of excess baggage. She has too much freight for the engine. Mr. Churchill's literary style lacks distinction; his characters have little vitality; his pages are lacking in humour and charm. But his books are discussions of subjects that interest the public at the moment when they appear; and they are an accurate mirror of public sentiment. The historian of the future could obtain a pretty good idea of "the state of the public mind" from 1900 to 1915 by reading them.

Strange and sad that he should have political ambition—wish to be a member of the legislature—aspire to success as a public speaker. America is in no need of politicians or of orators; what America needs is artists. It is more important that we should produce a great novelist, a great musician, a great poet, a great painter than it is for any one to be elected president. We can get along with any kind of a president; we have to; but we cannot get along

without artists. Men of letters and great artists are the lights of a nation; they are what
make it great; they are what give it a place in
history. Those who love their country ought
to rejoice more at the appearance of an original
literary genius than at any amount of battle-
ships or any number of "bumper" crops. Art
is more important than politics, because it is
concerned solely with those things that are eternal. One day John Morley met Dante Gabriel
Rossetti walking on the street; it was the very
day when a general election was in progress.
To the consternation of Mr. Morley, Rossetti
had not only failed to vote, but he was unaware
that an election was going on. Finally Rossetti
said, "Well, I suppose one side or the other will
get in, and I don't suppose it makes much difference which,"—and Mr. Morley now says that
although he was greatly shocked at the time, he
cannot for the life of him remember which *did*
get in, seeming to prove that Rossetti was right.
When Napoleon was trampling Germany under
foot, Goethe went right along producing novels,
lyrics, dramas; and time has proved the correct-

ness of his judgment. He could not take his mind off really important things for the sake of what was transitory.

Mr. Churchill has decided literary gifts. He can do much more for America by cultivating them than by joining the vast army of political workers.

Booth Tarkington has exactly what Winston Churchill has not—humour, charm, lightness of touch, a certain winsomeness of style as pervasive as sunshine. The difference between the two men is immediately apparent when we compare *Mr. Crewe's Career* with *The Gentleman from Indiana*. If we could make an amalgam out of Churchill, Tarkington, Harrison, Herrick, and Jack London, we should have a great American novelist; and every man of the five would make a distinct and valuable contribution to the fusion. *Richard Carvel* and *The Gentleman from Indiana* were published the same year, 1899, one a historical romance, in the correct fashion of the moment, the other a realistic portrayal of journalistic and political life in a small town. Since that date these two popular favourites have written side by side, unconsciously inviting comparative criticism. In choosing between them the public has taken both.

Such novels as *The Conquest of Canaan* (1905) and *The Guest of Quesnay* (1908) are good stories well told, without any other significance and without any permanent value. It is rather interesting that in the year 1915 our two novelists should each have produced a book that is intended to be, and is, an indictment of modern American conditions in the commercial life of big cities. Now there is surely more humanity in *The Turmoil* than in *A Far Country*. The hero of the latter novel is a mechanism merely, a representative of the evil tendencies condemned by the author; whereas in *The Turmoil,* both father and son are real persons, full of individuality. This story is a skilful accusation of the American love of bigness, with its concomitant evils of smoke, dirt, noise, especially noise. The son is as unlike his father as the sons of rich Americans are likely to be: in the end the enormous distance between them is

spanned by the longest bridge in the universe—
love.   The son is so much like the author of the
novel that we hope his apparent surrender to
big business at the end does not mean the surrender of Mr. Tarkington to the demands of the
reading public.   Four or five years ago I feared
that the brilliant gifts of this Hoosier were going
to be degraded to the production of the girl-
model of the year—he is much too able a writer
to become a caterer and to fall under the temptation of immediate success.   As the German
dramatist remarked when he wrote his first play
full of high ideals, ''The public is a Hydra'';
but when he found that the way to quick returns
was to please the public, he said cynically, ''The
public is not a Hydra; it is a milch cow.''   Many
of our novelists have discovered this truth; the
author gets from such a public rich payment
and bovine appreciation; as the cow chews its
cud in perfect contentment, so the healthy young
girls chew their gum as they turn the pages in
sweet delight.

The Turmoil is the most ambitious and on the
whole the best of Mr. Tarkington's novels; with-

out too much didacticism, it is an unsparing and honest diagnosis of the great American disease. Its author has proved that he can write a novel full of cerebration without losing any of his charm. In spite of that delightful miniature historical romance, *Monsieur Beaucaire,* Mr. Tarkington is a realist; he hates pretence, sham, cant in just the way a typical undergraduate hates them; perhaps if he did not hate them so much, perhaps if his sense of humour were not such a conservative force in his nature, he might attain to even higher ground. In his study of the American boy, *Penrod,* we see his shrewd knowledge of life and his original mirth-sense. The first half of the book is second-rate; it seems like a copy of some original; but the second half is wonderful, with its feeling for reality as against cant; and those two nigger-boys are worthy of Mark Twain at his best. The sense of fact is the dominant quality in Booth Tarkington, as it was in Mark Twain. It accounts for his artistic virtues, and for his lack of range. But *The Turmoil* proves that he is growing in spiritual grace.

Every man and woman over fifty ought to read *Seventeen*. It is not only a skilful analysis of adolescent love, it is, with all its side-splitting mirth, a tragedy. No mature person who reads this novel will ever seriously regret his "lost youth" or wish he were young again.

Perhaps it is natural that New York newspapers should have their jest at the expense of the so-called "Indiana School." For my part, I have for this group of writers only wonder and praise; wonder, that in the particular State of Indiana—why not in Illinois, Ohio, Kentucky, or Missouri?—a group of authors should appear, each of whom has an individual excellence; praise, because their actual merit, as compared with average American production, is so high. Edward Eggleston, Maurice Thompson, Lew Wallace, James Whitcomb Riley, Booth Tarkington, Meredith Nicholson, George Ade— these are all justly honoured names. And unlike as their personalities are, their work has one common distinguishing mark, literary honesty. Edward Eggleston's *Hoosier School Master* (1871) is a truthful picture of life, with

scenes and characters of extraordinary vitality.
I have not read the book for forty years, but at
this moment I can see the schoolmaster taking
off his coat to fight the husky Bud Means, and
the general surprise at the spelling-match when
the teacher was selected instead of the local
champion—wasn't his name Jeems Phillips?
Nor shall I forget my delight when I picked up,
fresh from the press, a copy of *Fables in Slang*,
and wondered who the author was, whether or
not George Ade was his real name, and if so,
how it was pronounced? Those *Fables* are
acute criticisms of American life. I venture to
say that entirely apart from their humour, they
constitute a more valuable handbook for fathers
and mothers who are worried about their children—and what ones are not?—than any of the
common moral treatises on the subject. I feel
sure that these *Fables* would be better for
school-teachers to study than many of the works
on pedagogy.

The flannel-shirted novelist, Jack London, has
never written anything nearly so good as his
Call of the Wild (1903), though the early chap-

ters of *The Sea Wolf* (1904) are brilliantly executed. When I began to read that story, the
scenes at the start, the tumbling into the icy
waters of the bay, the helplessness of the critic
of Poe's literary style in the presence of the
Wolf, I thought I was at last reading the great
American novel—but when I came to the love
scenes and the seal scenes, then I knew I was
not. During the great and fleeting popularity
of the "red-blood" school, an intense love of
which is a sure indication of effeminacy, Jack
London stood high in favour. Such phrases as
"red corpuscles" (whatever that may mean),
"male ardour," "sheer brutality," were quite
in fashion; indeed they were the dying kicks of
a pseudo-romanticism—instead of being a sign
of vitality, they were evidences of the last con-
vulsion. To read a book like *White Fang* is to
feel like a cannibal, crunching bones and bolting
blood. Yet Jack London is a man of letters;
he has the true gift of style, so rare and so unmistakable; if he would forget his social and
political creed, and lower his voice, he might
achieve another masterpiece. Meanwhile let us

be grateful for *The Call of the Wild,* a story that no other man could have written.

Is there a living writer more unlike Jack London than Robert Herrick? One born at San Francisco, the other at Cambridge—one a tramp by instinct and choice, the other a Harvard graduate and college professor. The last thing to say of Mr. Herrick's art would be that it lacked virility; but its virility is never forced on the reader, just as its author never shouts in public. His strength is a subdued strength; the virtues of his literary style are quiet; his literary attitude is ironical—of which the advertisement of fire-proof construction in the midst of the devouring flames is an excellent illustration. I sometimes think the best thing he has written is the short story called *The Professor's Opportunity.* It is a work of pessimism, a remorseless study of the sordid side of academical life, of the meanness of teaching, of the relations between the Assistant Professor who cannot live on his salary and the college President who is a liar—not a natural liar, but made perfect in deceit through the exigencies of

his office. The picture is not a pleasant one, and the emphasis is harsh, but those who read Mr. Herrick's novels for pleasure are bound to be disappointed. Wormwood, wormwood.

Every author has a right to surprise us by producing something "different"; but what did Mr. Herrick mean by writing *His Great Adventure?* This is a work worthy of the late Mrs. E. D. E. N. Southworth.

Of all American authors who have made their début in the twentieth century, I regard Mr. Henry Sydnor Harrison as the most promising. In January, 1911, no one had ever heard of him; by December everybody was talking about him. One novel, *Queed,* made the difference between obscurity and fame. I think *Queed* deserved all its success. It is a real novel, with a real plot, and real characters. The construction, the weakest point in most contemporary works of fiction, is particularly brilliant; from the first to the final bark of the pleasure-dog the story develops with naturalness. The only thing that seems like artifice is the too patent opposition of the clever young politician and the despised pedant; one increases in exact proportion to the other's decrease, so that at a certain moment they pass each other. But the hero is quite original in modern fiction, as original as Browning's *Grammarian* in poetry; all readers are stimulated by his spiritual advance.

The next book, *V. V.'s Eyes* (1913), despite its unpromising title, indicated no falling off. The conquest of a woman of the world by a Christian hero is not unknown in fiction, and was a favourite device in the novels of Dostoevski; it has been recently tried with success by Anne Sedgwick in *The Encounter;* its piquancy seemed to be felt by Bernard Shaw in *Androcles and the Lion*. The contrast has every dramatic possibility, and they are made the most of by Mr. Harrison. But apart from the main theme, this novel abounds in scenes of the liveliest humour and charm; scenes equalled for their truth in humorous details only by William De Morgan. Yet the real power of the book lies in its artistic handling of a great driving moral idea—the idea of Christian unselfishness, of the old paradox of saving one's life by losing it. The way in which countless little details are accumulated, every one of which aids in the development of the central thought of the book, is worthy of high praise. Mr. Harrison is something more than a clever novelist; he is a valuable ally of the angels.

His third novel, *Angela's Business* (1915), is distinctly inferior to its predecessors; inferior in construction, in characterisation, in human interest. It is too timely to wear the marks of permanence; and it completely lacks the freshness, the spontaneous charm of *Queed*. That novel was written apparently because the author could not hold on to it any longer; in writing it, he simply released something from his soul. Now, *Angela's Business* is the work of a professional novelist, from whom a new book is due; he selects his subject, and proceeds to cover white paper. There are, however, two notable features of this story which make me glad it was published; first, the leading lady is not the heroine. Angela deceives not only her family, her acquaintances, but what is much more difficult, she deceives the reader. Of course it is a favourite device of Mr. Harrison to present a character to his readers with a complimentary introduction, only to have the stuff depreciate on our hands; there is no sudden shock of disappointment or amazement, there is simply the slow change in our attitude from admiration to contempt—caused by a thousand details rather than by one catastrophe as in typical melodrama. The transformation is accomplished in a consummate manner. After reading the first chapter, no one would believe that this girl would or could develop as she does; yet at the end of the book both natural and moral values are correct.

The woman question—which no man can escape nowadays—is from one point of view finally disposed of here; which makes me regard *Angela's Business* as the best contribution to the whole question of feminism that I have seen in any work of fiction. It is much easier to write about woman than about woman-suffrage —that is, easier for a poet or a novelist; for woman-suffrage is not naturally malleable for purposes of art, while woman is and always has been an ideal subject. Mr. Harrison settles the question not from the point of view of feminism, but femininity; he proves to us that "womanly" women are so, not because of their occupation or because of their opinions, but because of themselves. An ardent suffragette may be full of delicate charm; and a frivolous woman may lack every vestige of attractive force. This ought to be axiomatic, but is not; Mr. Harrison's solution of the problem is not only the only correct one, but one that pros and antis should study with attention. As to whether or not women should have the ballot, Mr. Harrison leaves that question where he found it. His moral is that women need not fear to have opinions because of the danger of losing their charm —since many have neither opinions nor charm.

I have not read any book by Mr. Harrison without immediately wishing for another. He has won already an enviable place in contemporary literature, and of all our young writers, he seems to have the largest natural endowment.

Of our American woman novelists, Gertrude

Atherton and Mary Wilkins (Freeman) have
been before the public for about a quarter of a
century, and we know something of their range,
force, and quality. Mary Wilkins has shown
better judgment than Mrs. Atherton in sticking
closely to a certain field; narrowing her scope,
while gaining in intensity. If one picks out
almost at random from Mrs. Atherton's long
list of publications *Senator North* (1900), *The
Conqueror* (1902) and *Tower of Ivory* (1910),
one sees at a glance the almost impossible space
that this interesting and ambitious writer has
attempted to cover. Her personality is more
interesting than her novels; I find her "views"
and her pungent letters to the newspapers more
exciting reading than her formal works. She
would perhaps make a deeper impression on
contemporary literature if her novels hit the
same mark more often, if she were identified in
the public mind with some particular literary
manner, some artistic point of view—consider
the success of Eden Phillpotts, without mem-
tioning an original genius like Thomas Hardy!
Nor can I agree with Mrs. Atherton in her

spirited attacks on Mr. Howells and the American novel in general; for surely there is more actual truth in *The Rise of Silas Lapham* than in *Tower of Ivory*.

Many years ago I was invited to a literary "tea" in Boston, which confirmed my worst fears. Fourth and fifth class writers were present, each surrounded by satellites; other persons, of more ambition than capacity and more conceit than either, appeared in strange garments and talked in accents not of this world —one young man, I remember, wore a Greek gown! As George Moore would say, all that an ordinary man could do on beholding such a spectacle would be to shout *Great God!* and leave for some human destination. I was about to do this, when I saw in a corner a quiet, normal young woman, who was talking with a natural expression on her face. I enquired, and was told, "Oh, that's Mary Wilkins," as though she were the janitress. It was indeed Mary Wilkins; incomparably the most distinguished person in the room, looking as true to life as one of her New England characters.

Every line in the books of Miss Wilkins reads as though it had come out of the author's actual experience. She is primarily truthful, and never prepares an artificial effect—never sacrifices reality for sensation. Her novels are histories; histories of New England localities and of New England people. Such books as *Pembroke* (1894), *The Portion of Labor* (1901), and *The Shoulders of Atlas* (1908) are uncompromisingly faithful to fact. The last-named is indeed an experimental novel in the manner of Zola; just as honest, just as conscientious, just as unflinching as he. Only, while she represents the filth and sordidness of poverty, she also represents the love that dignifies and ennobles it. Religious aspiration and family love are exactly as "true to life" as the dirt on a man's boots—just as the unspeakable affection that exists between a man and a woman who have been married forty years, strengthened every day by the sight of each other's grey hairs, is as much of a fact as the animal passion that draws together young lovers. One cannot emphasise too strongly just now that a picture of life which is all sordidness is not a true picture; Gorki, for example, represents workers coming out of a factory with only one expression on every face, the sodden despair of hopeless weariness. But if one will stand at the gates of any factory in the world when the workers are released, he will see that Gorki is not telling the truth; they do not *all* have that expression, or look that way. There is plenty of misery in evidence; but many of the men and women act like boys and girls just let out of school; they are laughing, joking, and full of mirth. I request any fair-minded critic to read Gorki's *Mother* and Miss Wilkins's *The Shoulders of Atlas* consecutively, and then to declare which of the two novels is more true to humanity and to the facts of human existence.

At this moment Edith Wharton stands by common consent at the head of all living American women who write books; indeed there are many who say she is our foremost novelist. From this decision, handed down constantly in our magazines and reviews, I find myself forced to dissent. She has produced only one masterpiece, *Ethan Frome* (1911), giving only one aspect of country life, but presenting that in a wonderful technique. Yet even in this story I am unconvinced, for I am certain that the lovers never would have taken that coast to perdition; in real life they would have thought about it, as we all think of jumping off high places— without actually jumping. The story is, however, a grey masterpiece, a little group of miserable people living forever under a gunmetal sky.

Although *The Valley of Decision* (1902) attracted considerable attention, it was not until the appearance of *The House of Mirth* (1905) that Mrs. Wharton's popularity became general. Unlike most of her stories, no unusual intelligence is required to understand or to appreciate *The House of Mirth;* and no unusual intelligence was required to write it. A tale of exaggerated intensity, ending in melodrama. The two books that followed in 1907, *Madame de Treymes* and *The Fruit of the Tree,* illustrate the author's versatility; the former has great dignity, the latter none whatever. In-

deed *The Fruit of the Tree* is a failure, both
artistically and morally; we are evidently meant
to sympathise with the second wife, which is
impossible, because she is a murderer. I do
not refer to her overt act of murder when Bessy
was helpless, for there it is possible to admire
her courage in taking the responsibility; no, I
mean her reference to the wild horse in Bessy's
presence; the moment she mentions that dangerous beast, she is guilty of murder.

Next to *Ethan Frome,* I think Mrs. Wharton's
best novel is *The Reef* (1912); it has an excellent plot, and what is rare in her books, none of
the characters is overdrawn. As for *The Custom of the Country* (1914), as a work of satire it
is powerful, though immensely exaggerated;
and the scorn exhibited for American social
ideals and American social life shows exceed-
ing bitterness. Mrs. Wharton is a good hater;
if her sense of humour and her powers of human sympathy were developed in like measure
with her capacity for hate, disgust, and irony,
what a novelist she would be! She has all the
intellectual gifts, all the purely mental endow-

ment, without any spiritual force; there is from the first page to the last of all her novels that I have read no whisper of divine influence; positively no recognition of anything unseen and eternal; *she knows you not, ye heavenly powers!* I am not scolding her for this, I am merely mentioning it. Suppose she had even a touch of the spirituality and loving sympathy of Dostoevski, what a difference it would make in the manner of her work! Her range is limited by the boundaries of this world.

Apart from that vital loss in all her work, I find *The Custom of the Country* too overdrawn to be either a good novel or a really effective satire. If her purpose was to contrast American with foreign sentiment, one has only to remember Henry James's *American,* where the same task is accomplished in a more powerful way. After finishing *The Custom of the Country,* one really ought to read *The American;* I am sure that the contrast would be instructive.

Anne Sedgwick (Mrs. de Sélincourt) is a novelist who is attracting more thoughtful attention every year, and of whom Americans are becoming increasingly proud. She has had only one popular success, *Tante* (1911), a novel of strong dramatic quality, but decidedly inferior to *A Fountain Sealed* (1907). The two books have one thing in common, disillusion. What makes this writer so fond of the study of vampires? Tante is an artistic vampire; the young philanthropist is a moral vampire. What power of selfishness is displayed, what cruelty, what misconception of one's place in the universe! And what calm, intellectual joy Miss Sedgwick takes in very gradually stripping these goddesses! Where did she learn this particular art? who taught her such a lesson of bitterness?

In her novel *The Encounter* (1914) we have the philosopher Nietzsche as one of the leading characters. This extraordinary book has an absolutely negligible plot, almost no plot at all—indeed it is not a story, it is a problem. And the interest of the problem lies not at all in the incidents or in the course of events, but in the clash of character on character—really in the

clash of moral ideals. Only the other day a
clever American woman was asked what stand
she took on the American sale-of-munitions to
the Allies; and she replied sadly, "I don't know
where I stand on any question." There are
times when all the great questions of life seem
to leave honest persons in mere bewilderment;
happy are those who have no trouble in making
up their minds! The various kinds of *Anschau-
ungen* are illustrated in *The Encounter* by powerful personalities, whom the young girl actually encounters. Indeed, there are six characters in this story, every one of whom is going
to impress the reader—impress him so deeply
that he only half-misses the real absence of narrative. These are the young American girl
herself, whose mind has already received so
many impressions that it is just possible she
may be interested by a new one, but not possible
that any new one could produce shock; her
mother, a quite new person in modern fiction,
and yet strikingly real, with enormous power
of observation veiled by a mask of sleepy indifference—one feels sure that no individual has

ever penetrated to the quiet depths of this woman's soul; then there is the sentimental Italian devotee; Nietzsche himself, who is thought to be a superman, but who is really a great baby; Graf von Lüdenstein, with no philosophy except sensuality, knowing exactly what he wants, and without scruples, no Superman, but certainly a dangerous Subman; much more apt to live up to his desires than Christians are to live up to their principles, or philosophers to their ideals; and finally the cripple, Conrad Sachs, who represents without one word of cant, a living Christian faith translated into action. Sachs triumphs over the other two men, over the original contempt of the girl; indeed his conversations with the girl will make it impossible for any thoughtful reader to pass them lightly. They reach the depths of spiritual experiences. Conrad has charity for all, and immense admiration for Ludwig (Nietzsche); indeed, he says that Ludwig is really a Christian without knowing it, and that at any moment the truth may be revealed to him. For Ludwig insists that Strength is the highest good; Conrad merely makes an inversion, saying that Goodness is the highest strength.

This is a novel where every page betrays cerebration; one reads it with happy attention. And one rises from it convinced that the highest wisdom in life is not of the head, but of the heart. Seldom do we find a writer who combines such keen intellectual power with such spiritual sweetness.

Dorothy Canfield (Mrs. J. R. Fisher), who took her doctor's degree at Columbia in "Old French," made a happy substitution in changing her investigation from linguistics to American men and women of the twentieth century. In *The Squirrel Cage* (1912) she showed in a straightforward narrative exactly how our modern girls are systematically prepared for professional invalidism, for a long career of nervous prostration; in *Hillsboro People* (1915) she very nearly proved the paradox that you can learn more about human nature in a Vermont village than in New York City. This book also exhibited her skill in the short story. It is a series of tales, with lyrical intermissions by

Sarah Cleghorn, singing like linnets in the pauses of the wind. In her best and latest novel, *The Bent Twig*, solidly thoughtful and continuously interesting, we have another sound work of art. This time the life and ideals of a Middle-West State university are accurately, unsparingly, and affectionately portrayed. Dorothy Canfield is a notable addition to modern novelists, and each of her books marks a steady advance. I never prophesy, for prophecies are futile; but when I finished *The Bent Twig*, my attitude toward the author was and is now best described by the word Faith.

CHAPTER XI

HENRY JAMES

The adjective "Victorian"—the education of Henry James —his obscurity—his model and his influence—*The American*—*Daisy Miller*—the author's command of passion—a specialist—his verbose reticence—his uninteresting characters—his ghost-story—the beauty of his style.

THE word "Victorian" as applied to literary standards seems to have become little more than a contemptuous epithet; and there is in fact only one designation more insulting, which the reader at once correctly guesses to be "mid-Victorian." This twentieth-century attitude is rather interesting when we remember that there is not at this moment a single writer of either prose or verse in English who can compare in excellence with a half-dozen mid-Victorians that any book-lover can name.

Henry James was born on the fifteenth of April, 1843, and died at his lodgings in Chelsea on the twenty-eighth of February, 1916. As literary epochs go, it is a far cry to 1843; and

302

to Americans who love their country, and who
hope to see it take a position in the intellectual
advance of humanity, it is humiliating not to
be able to mention a single American prose
writer born since that date who is the equal of
the man we have lost. Of the splendid American triumvirate who lived to see the new century, Mark Twain, W. D. Howells, and Henry
James, only one is left, and he will be eighty
years old on the first of next March. I could
wish there were some form of literary "pre-
paredness" that would insure the United States
a place among world powers.

Henry James was metropolitan, cosmopoli-
tan, international; and he, with that all but infallible correctness of taste so characteristic
of his genius, selected for his birthplace the big
town where all roads of the world meet—New
York; and for his father a man who was novelist, philosopher, theologian, and who, like
Sainte-Beuve, passed through many intellectual
and religious phases; regarding both life and
death from a wide variety of mental stations,
possibly with the hope of getting ultimately a

correct parallax.   Henry and his great brother
William unconsciously received at tender age a
prophetic impulse; for Emerson laid his hands
on the future philosopher, and Thackeray
petted the future novelist.   Each had in maturity something of the manner commonly as-
sociated with the other's profession; William
succeeded in making the reading of metaphysics easy, while Henry made novel-reading difficult.

Henry's education, like that of John Mill and
Robert Browning, was largely under the personal supervision of his father; he was saved
from the waste and loss of our conventional
school system, receiving the incomparable advantages of Europe.   To be sure, Harvard has
the right to add his name to her illustrious roll,
for he was a student at the Law School in the
sixties.   His father never seemed to trouble
himself as to what Henry should "do"; like
Goethe, he perhaps thought that it was greater
to be than to do.   No one could have looked at
the face of Henry James when he was eighteen,
and have felt anything akin to anxiety; it was

a face that positively shone with intellectual beauty and nobility of spirit.

From first to last he seems to have followed what seemed to him to be the best things in life; from the year 1869 he resided chiefly in Europe, simply because he found there a more congenial mental environment, a sharper spur to artistic achievement. He would undoubtedly never have transferred his citizenship to England, if it had not been that England was in sore distress; the motive guiding this transfer was sheerly noble. Rightly or wrongly, he believed with all the strength of his mind in the British cause, yet this did not destroy his keen sense of moral values, for in a letter to the writer, dated December 15, 1914, he said, "Under this huge nightmare, the unprecedented oppression or obsession of our public consciousness here, pleasure (save of the grim sort that premonitions of Victory, terrifically paid for, bring) is very hard to take and very questionable even to desire." Since there was considerable unfavourable American journalistic comment on his change of allegiance, I do not think it imperti-

nent to quote a letter from an English novelist:
"He was a great personality in London, and
everybody who knew him seemed to have felt his
personal note, and of course in England we were
so immensely touched at his becoming one of
us in the darkest time our country has known
for centuries. It was the most supreme proof
he could give us of his sympathy and affection.
But his *own* country must not for a moment
think that he forgot it, for he didn't; and he left
directions, that his ashes, after cremation, were
to be taken back to it. There was much talk
of a service in Westminster Abbey, the Prime
Minister approved of it and the Dean was quite
willing there should be one, providing the Chapter consented (which was a matter of course).
But Mrs. William James, very wisely I think,
refused all idea of it. The simpler service in
the little church not a stone's throw from his
flat, was more in accord with his life, she said,
—better befitted a New Englander. So thus it
was; and a most beautiful and dignified farewell took place in the little church that is now

centuries old and will now be forever identified with him.''

The latest thing from his pen is his beautiful introduction to the posthumous letters of that overrated poet but not overrated man, Rupert Brooke. It is charming to see, as in the case of Gray and Bonstetten, the older man of letters captivated by the bright, eager youth. In this introduction, as in everything that he wrote, Henry James did his best. Never was there perhaps a writer of higher artistic purpose. When *The Ring and the Book* appeared, a reviewer remarked that Browning had done less to conciliate and more to influence the public than any of his contemporaries. The first of these propositions is certainly true of Henry James. So far as I know, he never betrayed any scorn for public opinion; he simply was not interested. He appealed always to the select few, to patient readers of trained perception, and his natural reward was that he had the followers that every writer would be happy to claim. He never had a large public, but he enjoyed a great fame. The target at which he aimed was so difficult that no wonder he frequently missed; but apparently he preferred even to miss rather than to shoot at something obviously easy. He took the credit, and let the cash go.

Excess of amenity will surely give a clever writer an immensely wide circle of readers, and yet the highest fame often comes to authors— as to statesmen—who defy the public. Lack of amenity may indicate a certain kind of courage, and while professional politicians are slow to learn it, the public really loves a display of courage. Browning is not always clear, but he is in the front rank of English poets; Hauptmann's vague *Sunken Bell* made him a world figure; Maeterlinck is obscure, but prodigiously admired; Ibsen is commonly regarded as the greatest of modern dramatists, and *The Master Builder* as a great play, yet no one can successfully demonstrate what it means. Do we not often reserve our highest tribute to the writers who refuse to help us overmuch? Perhaps if this is true, the reason lies in the fact that while it is pleasant to have our curiosity satisfied, there is one thing more stimulating —to have it aroused. An editorial writer on Henry James in *The Christian Science Monitor* summed the matter up rather neatly in one short sentence: "If he was not simple, neither were his times." He attempted to catch shades of meaning that are eternally elusive, that are perhaps quite beyond the reach of language, or, at all events, the English language:

> Thoughts hardly to be packed
> Into a narrow act,
> Fancies that broke through language and escaped.

Two common accusations—that he spent his time dealing in trivialities, and that "nobody reads him"—he admitted with cheerfulness, only he would have qualified the first by saying that he dealt in what seemed on a superficial glance to be trivialities. Mr. St. John Ervine —a novelist of marked talent—exclaimed, "I cannot read the works of Henry James. He seems to me to spend half a lifetime in saying 'Boo!' to a goose." But our author forestalled this objection long ago. So far as he had a model, it was the Russian novelist Turgenev, and it is clear that he highly esteemed Turgenev's praise. In his essay on Turgenev in *Partial Portraits,* he frankly confesses that the Russian was unable to read most of his productions. "As regards one of the first that I had offered him he wrote me a little note to tell me that a distinguished friend, who was his constant companion, had read three or four chapters aloud to him the evening before and that one of them was written *de main de maître.* This gave me great pleasure, but it was my first and last pleasure of the kind. I continued, as I say, to send him my fictions, because they were the only thing I had to give; but he never alluded to the rest of the work in question, which he evidently did not finish, and never gave any sign of having read its successors. Presently I quite ceased to expect this, and saw why it was (it interested me much), that my writings could not appeal to him. He cared, more than anything else, for the air of reality, and my reality was not to the purpose. I do not think

my stories struck him as quite meat for men.
The manner was more apparent than the matter; they were too *tarabiscoté,* as I once heard
him say of the style of a book—had on the surface too many little flowers and knots of rib-
bon.''

And unlike the newspapers that boast of their
enormous circulation, Henry James seemed at
times to be amused at the smallness of his
audience. The prefaces that he contributed to
the New York Edition of his works are full of
interesting comment, and one can hardly help
smiling at his candour in discussing the recep-
tion accorded to *The Awkward Age,* first published in *Harper's Weekly,* in the autumn of
1898, and brought out in book form the following spring. ''I had meanwhile been absent
from England, and it was not till my return,
some time later, that I had from my publisher
any news of our venture. But the news then
met at a stroke all my curiosity. 'I'm sorry to
say the book has done nothing to speak of;
I've never in all my experience seen one treated
with more general and complete disrespect.'

There was thus to be nothing left me for fond subsequent reference—of which I doubtless give even now so adequate an illustration—save the rich reward of the singular interest attaching to the very intimacies of the effort.''

Cooper was a romancer; Hawthorne an imaginative realist; Mr. Howells a realist; while Henry James is perhaps the best example of the psychological realist that we have in American literature. After all, Henry attempted in the concrete what William was forever trying in the abstract; William was constantly illustrating abstract ideas by concrete selections; Henry constantly attempted to make his persons illustrate shades of thought. Mr. Howells, with that royal generosity so characteristic of him, has paid many a noble tribute to his contemporary; but without subtracting one iota from Mr. Howells's merit, it is perhaps true that the younger man gave more to his friend than he received. The dates of publication, are, at all events, significant. I think it is true to say that the finest novels of Mr. Howells were published in the eighties, and the finest novels of

Henry James in the seventies. What are the best books of the former? Am I very wide in naming *A Modern Instance* (1881–82), *The Rise of Silas Lapham* (1884–85), and *Indian Summer* (1885–86)? And while the following choices will not please the devotee, is it not reasonable to select as Henry James's best titles to distinction, *Roderick Hudson* (1875), *The American* (1877), and *Daisy Miller* (1878)? And if you insist on *The Portrait of a Lady*, let us remember that it was published in 1881. Now while we cannot definitely say that Mr. Howells really owes anything to Henry James, for Mr. Howells has always gone his own way, there are two distinguished moderns of whom we can make the assertion with more confidence —Edith Wharton and Joseph Conrad. A writer has just reason to be proud of the admiration of such experts.

There is no doubt that the "later manner" is not an impressively successful improvement on the earlier; the later books are not only more difficult reading, they do not so richly reward the search; and I say this despite the fact that a Boston policeman told our novelist that his masterpiece was *The Golden Bowl*. Nór can I believe that the revised version—any more than in a more sacred illustration—is an improvement on the original. (The casual reader's suspicion here will be confirmed by the careful comparison made by Miss Clara McIntyre.) For my own part, I believe that as he descended into the vale of years, Henry James —possibly alarmed by the prevalence of journalistic phrases—became more and more afraid of obvious words. This is shown by his curious custom of placing quotation marks not merely around nouns, adjectives, and sentences immediately recognisable as current, but around many that have never been debased by vulgar use. Of course, he would now hate words like "message," "reactions," and "efficiency"; but in the preface to the revised version of *The Awkward Age* (1908), I counted fifty instances that seemed to him to require quotation marks; among others, "real" talk, its appealing "modernity," degree of the "sacrifice," on the "foreign" showing. All this, of course, is not a new tendency; it is a development of something discernible in his earliest work. The *Athenaeum* calls attention to a portion of a phrase on the first page of his earliest fiction, *The Story of a Year* (1865)—"Elizabeth (as I shall not scruple to call her outright) . . ."

To those who have lost their faith in Henry James, I can indicate a simple and all but certain way of recapturing it. Just reread *The American.* It is a work of genius, exhibiting a magnificent attack on an object that only very gradually is seen to be impregnable. The cheerful, indomitably confident, generous, big-hearted American is fighting against a foe whose strength he had never even imagined: the French idea of the Family Unit. Paul Bourget in his most earnest mood, his clever disciple Henry Bordeaux, in the highest reaches of his art—neither of these Gallic novelists has ever approached the distinctness or the tragedy with which our American writer has made his readers see his hero's defeat. An international novel like *The Custom of the Country* seems positively crude in comparison with this masterpiece. One has only to compare the profound truth of this great work of art—the clairvoyance of the author in his portrayal of the French point of view—with hundreds of "patriotic" works of fiction where the American enjoys a triumphal march across Europe, convincing both foreigners and home-bred readers that there is really no man on earth quite the equal of our youthful product, who combines marvellous athletic strength with chivalrous tenderness.

I was only a boy when *Daisy Miller* appeared; but I can distinctly remember the outraged cries of my elders. Daisy was "a libel on American womanhood." Of course, that is not the question; there is only one question, is she real? And if she had not been real, she could never have stirred such acrimonious debate. This book is not a novel, not primarily even a story; it is, as its author called it, a "study." It is a work of extraordinary analysis; it is really a diagnosis. The attitude of the author is one of strict impartiality. If in her freedom and innocent flirtation a "sharp

rebuke" was aimed at American girls who
travel abroad, so her splendidly unconscious
virginal purity might be called a rebuke to evil-
minded, suspicious, cynical Europeanised
Americans. Who comes off better under the
author's exploratory operation, Daisy or Winterbourne? And that last scene by the grave
—how much the subtle Italian has to teach his
American rival! "And the most innocent."
What immeasurable scorn is conveyed in those
words, and what echoes of vain regret are to
reverberate in the empty, polished corridors of
Winterbourne's mind!

I suppose if I should say that few modern
writers felt the terrible passion of love more
deeply than Henry James, I should be mentally
contradicted by the reader. Yet I believe the
remark to be true. Our author hated sentimentality and effusiveness of speech with ab-
horrence; but he meant thoughtful readers to
discover through his very chariness of language
the real depths of feeling. When Winterbourne
asks the Italian why he took Daisy to the
Coliseum, Giovanelli's reply, though spoken

most discreetly and without raising his voice, means "Because I had rather see her dead than married to you!" That the men and women in these novels do not indulge in verbal volcanoes is no sign that their insurgent hearts are not choking with passion. At the end of *The Princess Casamassima* young Hyacinth does not make a "scene"; but when he sees the cloak-model in an unmistakable attitude, he simply goes to his room and kills himself. Did the hopeless young man in *The Portrait of a Lady* know the tortures of love, or did he not? Has any other novelist made its cruelty more appalling? And we should have to go back to Browning's *Last Duchess* to find a woman whose daily life was so unutterably tragic.

Henry James was a specialist in art. Just as in the medical profession, we have general practitioners and specialists, so we find the same thing true in the history of fiction. Dickens was what I should call a general practitioner, handling all kinds of cases. Henry James was a specialist dealing with the finer shades of emotion, with peculiar patients suffering from a sickness quite beyond the ordinary novelist's range. He loves to isolate his American in a foreign environment where he stands out in sharper relief; if necessary, to darken the shadows around him, so that a powerful light may be played upon the object of the examination; for this reason he loved episodes rather than plots, sketches rather than full-bodied works. His own mind was so powerfully reflective and speculative that it would seem that he could not have been by nature a good observer; Meredith said that *The American Scene* was simply a tour in Henry James's inside. Yet our author has told us in one of his prefaces of the innumerable hours he spent tramping the London streets by day and night, and many of his travel impressions prove that little escaped him.

There are two qualities in the novels of Henry James that—quite apart from mere rhetorical difficulties—will probably always prevent his books from becoming popular. These are his reticence and his apparent lack of sympathy with his characters. There is something patrician about this reticence, something that a great democrat like Dickens not only could not have practised, but could not have understood; for Dickens has no reserve. Yet it is different from conventional reticence; and in an attempt to hit upon the right phrase to express it, I finally have decided to call the manner of Henry James a *verbose reticence.* All acts of the intellect and of the volition in the heroes and heroines of his later works are completely overlaid with wrappers and wrappers of language; yet the reader in the last extremity must always guess for himself, and never be quite sure that he has guessed accurately. In an honest attempt to tell us about the early days of his life, Henry James filled two fat volumes, out of which we get only a residuum of reliable information. This manner of course grows by what it feeds on; and it has made some of the later novels—to me, in the present stage of my development—simply unreadable, dense as a star-proof thicket. And in connection with this fact, I may add, that while Henry James's style at its best is most happily adapted to the subject, it is humorously inadequate for the expression of the simplest and most mundane wants. In *The Tragic Muse,* when the lovers are in a positive ecstasy by the water-side, the woman remarks, ''Detach the boat.''

Nor can the ordinary reader forgive the author for his apparent lack of sympathy with his characters. Daisy dies in half a sentence; more space is devoted to her parasol than to the outcome of her illness. One has only to remember Thackeray's sobbing out, ''I have just killed Colonel Newcome,'' to see the immense divergence in the point of view, in the novelist's attitude. Henry James, like a severely just parent, will not permit his affection for his literary children to obscure his vision of their characteristics. Indeed, I think in all his books, his sympathy for his men and women is displayed more by an intense and profound interest in all that they do and say, rather than by demonstrative tenderness.

Although in real life Henry James was much more interested in intellectual and cultivated folk than he was in commonplace and shallow people, this did not narrow his work. Some of his finest powers of analysis—some of his most skilful diagnoses—are displayed on unimportant, on uninteresting persons, if indeed there really be any such in the world. It is as though a great surgeon should devote all the assay of his art on hospital cases that could never pay. An excellent example of what I mean can be found in *Within the Cage,* where the telegraph girl is certainly not primarily either interesting or important—how wonderful that so eminent a novelist as Henry James should think her so supremely worth while! Nor can I find the mature characters in *What Maisie Knew* really worth to the casual acquaintance more than a passing nod. Yet they are apparently deeply absorbing to the novelist, and why? Because they mean so much to Maisie. A trivial caprice in any one of them might ruin or glorify the whole life of the little girl. I admire most of all in this book the wonderful consistency of the point of view. It really is "what Maisie knew"; every character, every speech, is presented to the reader as it is presented to the mind of the child. This perspective is honestly and consistently maintained; and I can only applaud the intellectual vigour required to "see it through."

After the unspeakable "kid-brother," Randolph C. Miller, the one altogether unlovely, whose pronunciation of the dog-letter rasps our nerves, and who has never been house-broken, I did not dream until the year 1898 that our author could draw a winsome, lovable, charming little boy, who would walk straight into our hearts. This year was a notable year in our writer's career; it saw the publication of *The Turn of the Screw,* which I found then and find again to be the most powerful, the most nerve-shattering ghost story I have ever read. The connoting strength of its author's reticence was never displayed to better advantage; had he spoken plainly, the book might have been barred from the mails; yet it is a great work of art, profoundly ethical, and making to all those who are interested in the moral welfare of boys and girls an appeal terrific in its intensity. With none of the conventional machinery of the melo-drama, with no background of horrible or threatening scenery, with no hysterical language, this story made my blood chill, my spine curl, and every individual hair to stand on end. When I told the author exactly how I felt while reading it, and thanked him for giving me sensations that I thought no author could give me at my age, he said that he was made happy by my testimony. "For," said he, "I meant to scare the whole world with that story; and you had precisely the emotion that I hoped to arouse in everybody. When I wrote it, I was too ill to hold the pen; I therefore dictated the whole thing to a Scot stenographer. I was glad to try this experiment, for I believed that I should be able to judge of its effect on the whole world by its effect on the man who should hear it first. Judge of my dismay when from first to last page this iron Scot betrayed not the slightest shade of feeling! I dictated to him sentences that I thought would make him leap from his chair; he short-handed them as though they had been geometry, and whenever I paused to

see him collapse, he would enquire in a dry
voice, 'What next?' ''

As the literary style of the novels of Henry
James has often wandered into what Hawthorne
called "the deep grass of latent meaning," I
should like to give—even at some length—an
example of what that style really was at its
best, and I shall select a specimen from one of
the novels, a specimen that shows the power of
its author in pure description. I take a passage from the revised version of *The Princess
Casamassima*. One day in London, while talking with Henry James, I remarked that many
passages in Browning which seemed obscure
to the eye became perfectly clear when read
aloud intelligently, and with the proper distri-
bution of emphasis. To my great surprise, he
whispered in my ear—there were others in the
room—this statement, whispered with intense
earnestness: "I have never in my life written
a sentence that I did not mean to be read aloud,
that I did not specifically intend to meet that
test; you try it and see. Only don't you tell."
I am sure that he will not mind now my calling

attention to this remark, because, if people who really know how to read aloud will try pages from his novels here and there, the result will often demonstrate their beauty, a beauty not always otherwise suspected. In order to enjoy the following selection, one must be not only a sincere lover of rural scenes, one must love nature partly for its human associations, with something of the unspeakable affection that Englishmen have for country "places" hallowed by generations of men and women. And the reader must try to see this vernal beauty with the eyes of young Hyacinth, who was as sensitive to loveliness as Keats, and who had not guessed there was much in life except the sordid squalor of the slums.

"Hyacinth got up early . . . an operation attended with very little effort, as he had scarce closed his eyes all night. What he saw from his window made him dress as quickly as a young man might who desired more than ever that his appearance shouldn't give strange ideas about him: an old garden with parterres in curious figures and little intervals of lawn that

seemed to our hero's cockney vision fantasti-
cally green. At one end of the garden was a
parapet of mossy brick which looked down on
the other side into a canal, a moat, a quaint old
pond (he hardly knew what to call it) and from
the same standpoint showed a considerable part
of the main body of the house—Hyacinth's room
belonging to a wing that commanded the extensive irregular back—which was richly grey
wherever clear of the ivy and the other dense
creepers, and everywhere infinitely a picture:
with a high-piled ancient russet roof broken by
huge chimneys and queer peep-holes and all
manner of odd gables and windows on different
lines, with all manner of antique patches and
protrusions and with a particularly fascinating
architectural excrescence where a wonderful
clock-face was lodged, a clock-face covered with
gilding and blazonry but showing many traces
of the years and the weather. He had never in
his life been in the country—the real country,
as he called it, the country which was not the
mere ravelled fringe of London—and there entered through his open casement the breath of

a world enchantingly new and after his recent feverish hours unspeakably refreshing; a sense of sweet sunny air and mingled odours, all strangely pure and agreeable, and of a musical silence that consisted for the greater part of the voices of many birds. There were tall quiet trees near by and afar off and everywhere; and the group of objects that greeted his eyes evidently formed only a corner of larger spaces and of a more complicated scene. There was a world to be revealed to him: it lay waiting with the dew on it under his windows, and he must go down and take of it such possession as he might.

"He rambled an hour in breathless ecstasy, brushing the dew from the deep fern and bracken and the rich borders of the garden, tasting the fragrant air and stopping everywhere, in murmuring rapture, at the touch of some exquisite impression. His whole walk was peopled with recognitions; he had been dreaming all his life of just such a place and such objects, such a morning and such a chance. It was the last of April and everything was fresh and vivid; the great trees, in the early air, were a blur of tender shoots. Round the admirable house he revolved repeatedly, catching every aspect and feeling every value, feasting on the whole expression. . . . There was something in the way the grey walls rose from the green lawn that brought tears to his eyes; the spectacle of long duration unassociated with some sordid infirmity or poverty was new to him; he had lived with people among whom old age meant for the most part a grudged and degraded survival. In the favoured resistance of Medley was a serenity of success, an accumulation of dignity and honour.''

Although there is little to report of external interest in the career of Henry James, I suspect few moderns have obtained more out of the precious gift of life than he. He lived keenly, he lived abundantly; and in his brave explorations on the frontiers of human thought and passion, I think he found many thrilling experiences, as thrilling as those of Drake and Columbus on uncharted seas. There is a memorable sentence in *The Sacred Fount,* a novel, that I suspect he meant as an Apologia. "For real excitement there are no such adventures as intellectual ones."

INDEX

[Only important references are given; the mere mention of names is omitted.]

Addison, J., a realist, 29; his style, 33; *Spectator*, 34, 57.

Ade, G., *Fables*, 282.

Allen, J. L., 268–271.

Atherton, Mrs. G., 290.

Austen, J., defence of novels, 8; *Northanger Abbey*, 88, 89; praises *Grandison*, 89; *Pride and Prejudice*, 91, 92, 121; *Persuasion*, 93; Elizabeth Bennett, 92, 97, 98; place in fiction, 118.

Balzac, H., *Père Goriot*, 26; compared with Smollett, 70.

Barclay, Mrs. F., *The Rosary*, 77.

Barrie, J. M., 223–225.

Bashford, H. H., 264.

Bellamy, E., 13.

Bennett, A., 156–159.

Blackmore, R. D., *Lorna Doone*, 19, 20, 23, 45.

Boyesen, H., remark on *Middlemarch*, 114.

Bradshaigh, Lady, correspondence with Richardson, 60, 76.

Brontë, A., *Agnes Grey*, 118.

Brontë, C., 118–121.

Brontë, E., *Wuthering Heights*, 118, 119.

Browning, R., compared with Richardson, 48, 51; *My Last Duchess*, 115.

Bunyan, J., *Mr. Badman*, 35.

Bulwer-Lytton, E., choice of Scott's novels, 101.

Burton, R., *Anatomy*, 57; his love of coarse fun, 68; influence on Sterne, 74.

Butler, S., *Way of All Flesh*, 232–241.

Canfield, D. (Mrs. Fisher), 300.

Cholmondeley, M., 262.

Churchill, W., *Inside of the Cup*, 4, 14; *Richard Carvel*, 148; general criticism, 273–277.

Clifford, Mrs. W. K., *Love Letters of a Worldly Woman*, 261.

Collins, W., *Woman in White*, 104, 121; his work, 121–123.

Conrad, J., 192–217.

Cooper, J. F., compared with Richardson, 55; his heroines, 94, 96, 97; his vitality, 102, 103; compared with Conrad, 211.

Cowley, A., master of prose, 30; specimen of his style, 32; personal essays, 57.

Date Due